THE MAN OF MANY FATHERS

THE MAN
OF MANY
FATHERS

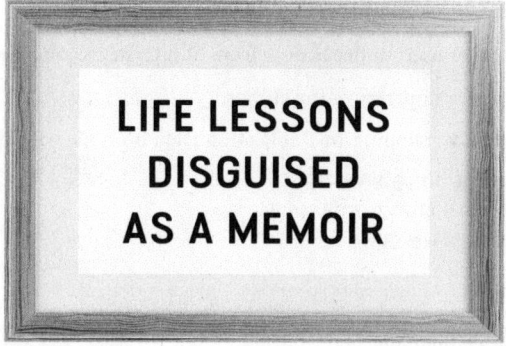

LIFE LESSONS
DISGUISED
AS A MEMOIR

ROY WOOD JR.

 CROWN
NEW YORK

CROWN
An imprint of the Crown Publishing Group
A division of Penguin Random House LLC
1745 Broadway
New York, NY 10019
crownpublishing.com
penguinrandomhouse.com

Illustrations by Kashmir Thompson

Picture-frame images used under license from Shutterstock.com/iunewind.

Photograph on page v courtesy of the author.

Library of Congress Cataloging-in-Publication Data is on file with the publisher.

Hardcover ISBN 978-0-593-80007-2
Signed edition ISBN 979-8-217-08846-1
Ebook ISBN 978-0-593-80008-9

Editor: Matt Inman
Assistant editor: Fariza Hawke
Production editor: Natalie Blachere
Text designer: Andrea Lau
Production: Heather Williamson
Copy editor: Elisabeth Magnus
Proofreaders: Sasha Tropp and Robin Slutzky
Publicist: Tammy Blake
Marketer: Chantelle Walker

Manufactured in the United States of America

1st Printing

First Edition

The authorized representative in the EU for product safety and compliance is Penguin Random House Ireland, Morrison Chambers, 32 Nassau Street, Dublin D02 YH68, Ireland, https://eu-contact.penguin.ie.

Trying to raise a child before healing
your inner child is a motherfucker.
I've tried to pass down the best of you and discard the rest.
Thank you for trying.
Your son.

CONTENTS

THE MAN OF MANY FATHERS

A Letter to My Son

Dear Son,

It must have been 2006, maybe 2007, about ten years before you were born, when I ran into actor and comedian Brandon T. Jackson on Father's Day in Chicago's Midway Airport. I didn't know Brandon that well at the time, but we were both on the Los Angeles comedy scene pretty heavy. We stopped and spoke to one another. Had we seen each other anywhere in Los Angeles, this same moment would've warranted nothing more than a brief head nod out of respect.

But stand-up comedy is such an isolating, nomadic life, especially on travel days. When you see another comedian in the airport it feels good, even if you don't know them that well. You are in a place with thousands of strangers, and you have found the one person who understands *exactly* what you're going through. A moment that would be a passing head nod on the streets of Hollywood becomes a full-on conversation in an airport.

Brandon and I talked while walking to one of the little airport convenience stores. Like most comedians, we commiserated over our industry gripes and career challenges. "Drama bonding" is what I like to call it. I was struggling financially after taking a moral stance against a comedy club booker who accounted for 40 percent of my road bookings. Brandon, meanwhile, was in the middle of multiple auditions for a pretty major comedy film. He was nervously optimistic he would get the role but also worried about what booking the film would mean for his availability for the more reliable television roles during that same time. I politely poked and prodded him for more information about the film to help him weigh the pros and cons, but all he could tell me was "It's a comedy with Ben Stiller."

Once inside the store, Brandon made a beeline to the greeting-card rack and began frantically looking through what was left of the Father's Day options on sale. The rack was barren like grocery store shelves when people make a run for the milk and bread before a hurricane. Between topics, Brandon would pull a Father's Day card off the rack, read it, then ask me for my opinion on the prose inside the card.

"Getting this to my pops as soon as I land—I want a card that really says something," he said, while handing me a card. "What do you think about this one?"

My responses lacked the reassurance he was looking for, so he'd put each card back on the rack and search for another. We did this for about three or four greeting cards, and every time my reaction was the same. Humdrum. Take it or leave it.

Brandon got frustrated and looked at me like a date who couldn't decide where to eat. He fired off sarcastically, "Well, damn, what kind of card do you get *your* father?"

I thought about it for what was probably far too long and replied, "I don't think I have ever bought a Father's Day card."

Brandon froze. It was one of those moments when you know you could ask a follow-up question if you wanted, but you also don't know where the answer is going to take you and you've got a flight to catch.

Presumably pressed for time, Brandon passed on a follow-up, and the conversation returned to the usual industry fodder. Shortly thereafter, we shook hands, said our goodbyes, and headed off to our respective gates. Back to the comforting isolation that is traveling for a living.

I have never forgotten that conversation.

It was the first time as an adult when I actually had to stop and think about what my relationship with my father was like. Thank God Brandon was running late for his flight. There's no telling how I would have answered his follow-up question.

In the sixteen years that I knew him, I'm positive I bought gifts for my father here and there, but I truly cannot recall ever buying him a card, for Father's Day or for any other holiday. I can't even recall making him one of those terrible arts-and-crafts mugs that public school teachers always think are a good idea.

The masculine culture that I was immersed in was full of confidence building and discipline. Rarely was it full of compassion and gentleness. There were more handshakes than hugs. I can count on one hand the truly sentimental moments I've had with my father—or any male relative—or any man.

When I was growing up in the South, consistent male role models were far and few between for me. Both of my grandfathers were dead and gone long before I was born. I didn't have my first male teacher until the seventh grade. In the early days, my father came in and out of my life like the next-door neighbor on a wacky sitcom. It'd be fourth grade before we settled in under the same roof and I received anything that resembled consistent contact. It would be only eight years later when we would talk for the last time.

Son, when you were born, I went through something that day. Having a child is interesting because the first thing you do is think about all of the things you're going to do with them, the way you're going to throw a ball together or learn chess together. You start making plans for education and social engagement. "I'm so full of knowledge!" you excitedly think to yourself. "Which piece of knowledge will I pass down to him first?" After those feelings subside, you think about how you are going to teach this child values. That, in turn, forces you to think about how *you* were taught values—to audit your own parents.

I sat back in the delivery room just holding you and thought about the time that I had with my father, who died when I was sixteen. I didn't feel like I got as many lessons from him as I plan to give to you. And I did not like the report that I was beginning to put together. With my dad, there were some highlights, but there were for sure a few things missing. The more I thought about simple life lessons I wanted to teach you, like the value of saying please and thank you and "Yes, sir" and "No, sir," the importance of chivalry, and my approach to avoiding violent situations, the more I realized I did not learn most of these things from my own father. I learned these lessons from other men who came in and out of my life.

After my father's death, I was an enraged and isolated sixteen-year-old determined—and then forced—to figure things out on his own. They say it takes a village to raise a child, and my village has stretched almost forty years. As I sat in the delivery room holding you in 2016, I reflected on how lucky I have been to have so many men over the decades who have imparted wisdom, either knowingly or unknowingly.

I've set out to tell the stories of these moments because each of them is an important thread that's been woven into the fabric of fatherhood in which I now envelop you, son. I did not start interacting with many of these men until later in life. God willing, you will meet twice as many before the fourth grade.

I think this is why I'm not a fan of Father's Day greeting cards. They rarely encompass the complexities of parenting and mentorship. Every card is written from the assumption that a father is completely loved and has gotten everything right, which always makes me laugh. This could not be any further from the truth. Father's Day would be better served if there were cards that simply thanked a man for what you specifically learned from him, good or bad.

"For the dad who taught me how to avoid drug dealers."

"For the dad who showed me the importance of choosing the right partner."

"For the dad who saw me sleeping in my car that one time at a truck stop and gave me a solution to my problem."

These are the kind of cards that I believe would fly off the shelves.

That's why I'm going to jump at any opportunity to get worthy men in front of you as soon as possible. Fatherhood is a job that's bigger than any one man.

Parenting is one part instilling in your children what you believe to be the best of you and one part recognizing what is the best in your child and watering those parts of them. We sometimes make the mistake with our children of trying to turn them into the things we wish we were without identifying why we wish that change for ourselves. But to identify the best parts of yourself, you will have to identify the worst parts of yourself too. I held you tighter in the delivery room as I contemplated this self-audit. That's the hardest part of parenting: figuring out how to heal your damage and protect your child from suffering the same damage, all while figuring out how you became that damaged in the first place.

I've decided to take a break from parenting to write this book for you and tell you about some of these men and the lessons I learned along the way. Tales of my highs and lows in the entertainment and journalism worlds will have to wait. As will stories featuring the many women who helped me become a man. Today I'm only here to write about one woman—my mother—and a bunch of the men.

It is their wisdom that I will use to help construct a village for you, so that one day when you finally meet Brandon T. Jackson in an airport, you'll know exactly what kind of Father's Day card to help him find.

Love,
Dad

P.S.: Brandon booked the movie. When you get a little older, son, check out *Tropic Thunder*. Still a classic.

CHAPTER 1

The Doo-Doo Green
Cutlass Supreme

There's no honest way to begin this book about fatherhood without first talking about my mom, Joyce. Two of the most important tools I possess as a man came from her: compassion and toughness.

They say a scent can remind you of someone. Something as simple as a flower, a summer breeze, the smell of baked cookies. I can't have a hot dog without thinking of her. I love eating those diced-up bits of multiple animals encased in a pork sleeve and seasoned with all types of carcinogens outlawed by the EPA and USDA because they make me feel closer to the woman who raised me.

My early memories as a child are of me being a latchkey kid in Memphis, Tennessee. My mother had separated from my father in early 1979, not even a year after I was born, and left him behind in New York City to head to Memphis to pursue her graduate degree and be closer to her family in her hometown of Clarksdale, Mississippi. My earliest memories as a child do not include my father. It was just me and my mom and me watching her trying to make things work.

My mother was tough and afraid of no one. In undergrad, she had been among the first wave of Black protesters at Delta State University who organized sit-ins at the president's office demanding better conditions for Black students on campus. She would then take this same tenacity over to Florida A&M University as a grad student.

I always looked forward to breakfast with my mom. When she ate, her mind slowed down. I could see the problems and stresses leave her as she sat and enjoyed her food. A good meal was her departure from this world for a moment. Breakfast was also when we talked the most.

But some mornings we would be late getting out of the house, so we'd have to get creative about breakfast and the car would double as a kitchen table. My mother had a 1975 Oldsmobile Cutlass Supreme. It was doo-doo green with white bucket seats and a custom ragtop white roof to match. This was the age before center consoles in cars, so there was a full three feet of open seat between me and my mother. This is where I set up our breakfast spread. Some days we would eat plated foods like eggs or waffles, but we soon discovered one food in the house that's the simplest and most efficient: the hot dog. I would lay out four slices of bread, and on top of each I would place a piping hot, freshly boiled hot dog. Motor vehicle laws dictated that a kindergartener should be in the back seat, but since I was in charge of assembling the hot dogs for her, I got to sit up front. Those days were the best.

After my mother dropped me off at school, she'd work long hours in administration at Memphis State University by day, then go straight to grad school at night. A regular babysitter was a luxury that came and went like the wind, and most of the family members willing to chip in for free were an hour away in Mississippi, so if my mother was tight on money, she'd leave me home alone after school—with one instruction. "Don't answer the phone, don't answer the door!" she'd say to me, the kindergarten student.

Next to the phone was a list of "emergency numbers," which was just a list of coconspirators ready to speed over to the house and meet my needs to keep me from being swooped up by child protective services. At the top of the list was Olivia, one of my mother's college friends. She came over to the house often. The rest of the people, as far as I could tell, were a mix of coworkers and church members. As the old African proverb goes, "It takes a village to keep a single mother from losing her child to the system."

Like most latchkey kids, I was saddled with making my own dinner sometimes. By first grade, I was well versed in the preparation of franks and beans, pot pies, TV dinners, waffles, bacon, cold-cut sandwiches, and of course, the good old-fashioned American hot dog. I learned how to use a stove before I learned how to shoot a basketball. I wasn't a full-blown chef or anything, but my mother gave me enough skills to know that she didn't have to worry about me ever starving to death in her absence.

I never "missed" my dad per se during the Memphis years. When your first memories don't include a father in the home, you do not know that you're missing a father in your home. Sometime when I was in the first grade, my father left his job in New York City at WCBS to become the news director of a Black-owned radio station in Birmingham, Alabama. Closer to me in Memphis, he made the three-hour drive to visit us about once a month.

Just because your father is far away doesn't mean he can't touch you. My father was a tall man, about six foot three, with a deep voice that could shake paint off the walls and huge hands that, when raised to the sky, could eclipse the sun and the moon.

I remember one day, my mother was on the phone with him and trying to slice an orange for me at the same time. She was taking too long, so I snatched the knife away from her and told her that I could do it myself. I *insisted.*

My mother handed me the sharp, serrated steak knife and took a step back. She grinned. I'd watched my mom slice an orange many times. How hard could it be? I knew how to hold the knife just fine. What I hadn't paid attention to was where my mother placed her other hand while holding the orange. My thumb was under the blade and as I sliced down into the orange, I sliced my finger wide open.

White meat dangled from the open wound. I screamed as blood streamed out of my thumb and down my arm. To make matters worse, stinging acidic orange juice raced inside the cut to replace the blood that was streaming out of it. While getting a paper towel, my mom handed me the phone. "Your father would like to speak with you," she said with a sly grin. As soon as I put the phone up to my ear, my father did not disappoint. His voice rattled my brain and shook the earwax free in my ear canal.

"Goddamn it, boy! Didn't your mother tell you to wait? Now look at you!" he screamed. "You don't know everything yet!"

His words rattled me down to my core like an acoustic earthquake. The shockwaves from the booming bass in his voice created pure shock and awe. He hit me with the ferocity of a baseball manager yelling at an umpire who'd missed a call. When your child messes up, parenting usually boils down to either "Scold, then comfort" or "Comfort, then scold." My dad's strategy somehow was "Scold, then scold some more, then comfort a week later."

His booming voice was more than enough to make me forget that I probably needed stitches. I was crying now, not because of the pain but because I knew I was in trouble with my father.

Conversations like this encouraged me to stay on my best behavior because once a month, I knew the boogeyman was going to drive over from Birmingham and I didn't want to be on his bad side that week. And for the most part, I was a good kid. But try as my mother might to keep me that way, there's only so much a single mother in grad school can do on her own. The phone calls and occasional visits from my dad helped, but none of it was enough to stop me from slipping into an addiction to a drug called freedom.

■ ■ ■

To this day, I am stubbornly married to the idea of not needing anyone to get things accomplished. Being a latchkey kid planted the idea in my head very early on that I did not require an adult to function in this world.

Every now and then, starting in first grade, I'd take some of my allowance and pig out on candy. I had a bike by this point, so I could take a ride to the front of the apartment complex where there was a corner store. Rather than save up the money to buy a major toy, I would just go and eat Laffy Taffys. My mother wasn't crazy about it, but it wasn't that big of a deal. I generally would eat as much candy as I could before I got home, knowing that any candy I brought with me into the house would be governed by my mother. This did not stop me from sneaking candy at home, though.

To my mother's credit, she tried to keep our home free of snacks and candy and ice cream. These were treats for special occasions and her tools for behavioral manipulation. So for her to find candy wrappers in the house was serious business, like contraband-in-prison serious. And mothers are always the best forensic investigators.

Each night, I had to be smart about getting my candy in before I heard her walk in the door. Lying in bed, I knew her routine just by the sounds. She'd come in the door, make a beeline for the kitchen, and put her keys and purse on the counter. Then she'd hop on the phone to call a girlfriend. I couldn't make out much of what my mother was saying, but between murmurs, you'd hear occasional eruptions of laughter. Whatever they were talking about, it must have been fun and uplifting because she called her friend every night. My mom has a smile that can light up an entire city and a laugh that could wake an entire county. She was loud, and I loved it. I never knew what made her so joyful and free, but it was interesting to experience such a different side of my mother every night, even if only from afar.

One night I was awakened from my sleep to the loud cackles coming from my mother downstairs. I don't know who she was on the phone with, but they were having a good-ass time. Then suddenly laughter stopped.

"Girl, let me call you back," she said sternly. Something was wrong.

She hung up the phone. *Hard.* Then I heard her slam the lid to the trash can. *Hard.* That's when I knew . . .

Fuck! The wrappers! I snuck candy in the house, then threw the wrappers away in the fucking communal trash can! *Fuck fuck fuck fuck fuck fuck fuck fuck!*

My heart began to race. Next, I could hear her stomping up the stairs. We had carpeted stairs, so you really had to try to make noise on them. I quickly repositioned my body to pretend I was asleep. I hoped that she would barge in and see me sleeping peacefully and push this issue to tomorrow's morning agenda when she was a little calmer.

Wrong.

Standard operating procedure on nights like this was for my mom to turn the lights on and snatch the covers off me. Shock and awe. The glare of the bright lights, plus the temperature change, plus her yelling, were a lethal combination to extract the truth. She never had to lay a hand on me. She'd talk loudly, talk fast, and demand I open my eyes so the light could pour into them.

Even if I'd wanted to lie about what happened, I didn't have enough time to think of a good lie. Her routine was no different this time. She flipped the lights. "Get yo ass up!" she yelled.

For some reason, once the lights came on, I wasn't scared anymore. I ripped my covers off before she even had a chance to get to me. It threw her off. But she stormed over and held the wrapper of a Laffy Taffy in my face.

"What is this!? Who told you you could have candy all times of night?" she screamed.

She held it in my face like a wife who'd found a condom wrapper in the car. She did the classic "hold it so close to my face I can't even read it" move.

"I asked you a question, boy! Who told you you could have candy in this house?"

"Nobody!" I screamed back.

"Well, what's it doing here?" my impromptu drill sergeant screamed back.

"Because I wanted candy!"

"Well, you can't have candy in this house!"

"Well, why not? I do everything I'm supposed to do, I do all my chores, I eat all my vegetables, I brush my teeth, so why can't I have candy?"

"Because that's the rule in *my* house."

"Well, this house sucks."

"Well, you're welcome to find another house! If I catch you sneaking candy in here next time, it's gon' be the belt!" she screamed.

My mother turned the light off and left my room as quickly as she came. She was a total verbal and sensory tornado. The entire exchange had taken less than thirty seconds. I probably hadn't said my piece in the right tone, but I meant what I said, and it was the first time I'd ever told a grown-up the truth about how I felt. I must give my mother credit for letting me be honest, even if she didn't agree. That night changed our relationship for the better to this day. I knew I could tell her the truth about my feelings and not be punished for them as long as I spoke respectfully. Punish me for what I did? Sure, but punish me for my feelings? Never.

The moment had passed, but for some reason I was still *pissed.*

"Find another house." My mother's words kept echoing in my mind.

She'd tried the same shit with me at Southland Mall about a year earlier. My mother constantly needed a new pair of pantyhose and was stuck in a never-ending loop of going to department stores like M. M. Cohn and Goldsmith's. If we had enough time, she would let me go to the toy store so I could gawk at the latest toys that were coming out.

I was in the toy store and I saw the Holy Grail of toys, the Voltron Black Lion. Voltron was the predecessor to the Power Rangers, a bunch of smaller color-coded lion robots that joined together to form a larger robot that yielded a large sword and defeated alien monsters. The Transformers also had a line of robots that could join together to form a larger robot, but none of them were as cool as Voltron. The Black Lion was the leader of the group and thus was always the hardest one to get because it was never in stock. Not only was *Voltron* my favorite cartoon, but I knew the Black Lion would be my favorite toy. It was the only thing I'd wanted for two years, and I begged my mother for it. She simply said, "No."

"We don't have the money for that kind of stuff," she'd mumble under her breath to make sure that the white cashier did not hear her admitting to not having money.

I tried to stress to her how unlikely it was that the Black Lion had appeared at all. These were the days when stores legitimately did not know when they would get more items in stock. Just because the store had the item today didn't mean that the truck next week was going to bring more of it. Most of the time, if you wanted to save yourself the trouble of driving to that location, you literally had to call store after store after store to find a particular item. We were decades away from the luxuries of simply clicking on a website to see which store near you has the item in stock.

The Voltron Black Lion was as hard to get as Beanie Babies, Tickle Me Elmo, a PlayStation 5, or Beyoncé tickets, and there it was, *there* on a shelf, ready to be purchased. And my mother said, "No." I was furious, but there also wasn't much I could do about it.

I followed her out of the toy store screaming and crying that it wasn't fair. We got about halfway through the mall before I planted my feet at the center fountain and refused to move. My logic was, if I made enough of a scene, she would acquiesce and give me what I wanted for the sake of not being embarrassed. What I did not realize was that my mother was impervious to embarrassment.

As I wailed she squatted down to my eye level and said, calmly, "Keep yelling and screaming like this, I'm going to leave you in this motherfucking mall."

Challenge accepted, Joyce.

So I screamed even louder. My mother politely stood up, gathered her purse and shopping bags, straightened up her hair, and walked toward the exit. At this point we had the undivided attention of everyone in the mall. The farther away from me she walked, the louder I cried.

"I want the lion! Give me the lion!"

It is important to note that I had never done this before with my mother. I was not that kind of a child. I was rather calm, but this was the Voltron Black Lion, so I pulled from the playbook of what I had seen white children do to their parents in the mall. It had worked like a charm for them.

I, however, was having some difficulties running the same play. My mother did not come running back to me. She didn't even look back over her shoulder. She just calmly walked away as if she didn't even have a child.

Finally, a white woman intervened. She hustled to keep up with my mother as she stated the obvious to her.

"Excuse me, miss, excuse me, miss, but I think you left your son."

My mother ignored the woman and continued at her relaxed pace. She even looked at the white woman with a blank expression on her face as if she did not speak English.

"Miss! Miss! You're leaving your son!"

Another Black woman intervened.

"Mind ya business, you old nosy bitch! She know she left him."

My mother walked out the doors of Southland Mall and disappeared into the sea of cars in the parking lot, and there I stood in the mall food court, alone.

I suddenly stopped crying and my first thought was, *Did she just leave me at the mall? Oh my God, I'm alone at the mall! I'm alone!*

The horror of being alone finally set in. What had originally been just a manipulative temper tantrum suddenly evolved into real fear, and real tears. The white woman squatted down and tried to wipe my tears. I swatted her hand away, still unsure if I could trust strangers.

"Well, at least tell me your name, sweetie. We're going to find you a safe place to sleep tonight."

I looked over her shoulder and saw a car slowly come into focus. As the car crept up slowly to the curb, identity confirmed, a 1975 doo-doo green Cutlass Supreme, with my mother behind the wheel. She tooted the horn two times and made a motion for me to come get in the car.

I sprinted toward that car like it was the last rescue helicopter in a war zone. The last thing I remember as I ran toward the doors of the Southland Mall was that same Black woman taking one more shot at the white lady.

"See, she was never gonna leave that baby, he just needed to get his shit together. This why you should mind your business, you old nosy hoe!"

I don't even remember opening the car door. I was so scared of being left at the mall, I must've leapt in. I was defeated. I hadn't gotten the Voltron toy, and I'd lost the battle of wills. My mother had this stupid smirk on her face—a smirk that said, "You've got a lot to learn." Knowing what I know now, what I was feeling was the desire to be independent, the desire to not need anyone.

That incident at Southland Mall was all that ran through my mind as I lay in bed looking at the Laffy Taffy wrapper still sitting on the ground. It lay there like debris after the storm that my mother had come in and instigated.

Less than five minutes after storming into my room, my mother was back downstairs on the phone laughing and smiling, after an *obviously* unjust attack on me for daring to have a treat *that I'd paid for,* in her house. It's *my* money, but it is *your* house. Which takes precedence? I needed a lawyer to decide this, but I couldn't afford one.

From the sound of her voice, I knew she had that smirk on her face again.

What she'd said that night in the room again ran through my mind. "Find another house."

I lay there and thought to myself, *You know what, Joyce? Maybe that is exactly what the fuck I'm going to do.* I stood up, turned the lights on, and started packing.

Fuck you, I'm out of here.

I did not know where my mother kept my luggage. Most of the time when I was sent down to Mississippi, all my belongings were in a large duffel bag, but there was no time to look for any of that shit. I had to hit the road *now.* I knew for sure that the plastic bag that came with the candy I'd bought was still in the trash can downstairs. Perfect.

I got dressed and headed downstairs. My mother was on the phone laughing and having a good old time as I walked into the kitchen clearly dressed to leave the house. She looked at me briefly, laughed, and went back to her phone conversation. This infuriated me even more.

Southland Mall all over again.

But this time I was ready. *It's on, motherfucker.*

I took the plastic bag out of the trash, went upstairs, and got everything I needed for my trip: a pair of Star Wars pajamas and two pairs of underwear. That's it. Pajamas and underwear. I headed back downstairs and hit the kitchen for a few snacks for my trip: an orange Hi-C juice pack and a Twinkie. I wasn't sure if this was everything I'd need for my trip, but at this point the plastic bag was filled to the brim. I grabbed my bicycle, and made my way to the door.

This charade had gone on for too long, and my mother finally decided to say something.

"Girl, hold on a second, this little nigga at the door holding a Twinkie. Roy, where you going?"

"I'm not telling you."

"Okay, well, have a good trip."

She said this, then turned her back on me. I was motherfucking *fuming*! She refused to debate me. She refused to engage with me. *How dare you!* I exited the apartment and headed out into the street.

I hopped on my bike and hit the streets of Coventry Creek. The apartment complex was blanketed by trees so high and thick that they'd practically grown over the streetlights.

Nightfall brought an unnatural level of darkness to Coventry Creek that not even city lights or the moon could permeate. It was dark and scary, but I was determined. I sped past the guard's booth and the only words he could muster were "Boy, where the hell are you going at nine at night?"

I didn't reply; I wasn't in the mood for answering to authority.

I emerged on Winchester Road when it finally occurred to me, *Where* am *I going?*

My mother had this one college friend who lived around the corner from us, Olivia. When I say "around the corner," I mean about a mile and a half, which is far for an eight-year-old at nine at night on a bicycle that's weighed down with Twinkies and pajamas. So, considering I had no fucking way to know how to get to Highway 61 to ride all the way to Mississippi, and Olivia's apartment was the only place I knew how to get to from memory, I set course for Olivia's apartment.

I huffed and puffed the ten minutes to Olivia's place and banged loudly at the door. Through the door I heard blues music playing. The door slowly cracked open to reveal a tall, scrawny, Black woman with a corded house phone in one hand, a Winston cigarette in the other. She looked over me with a knowing smile.

"*Mmm* hmm, it's him. He just got here. . . . Okay, see you in a minute, Joyce."

Olivia put the phone down and squatted down to my eye level.

"Boy, what the hell you doing here?"

"I ran away," I said.

Olivia cracked a smile and took a long drag from her cigarette and said, "I know you ran away; I asked you what the hell you doing *here*? Why you bring yo ass over *here*? Your mama figured this is where you were coming. Hell, you don't know the way to anywhere else but school and McDonald's, and both of them closed. Now get your ass in this house before we both get robbed."

It had been a hard ride over to Olivia's, so I was ready to kick back with my Twinkie. Hearing the wrapper, Olivia didn't even turn around to address me with eye contact.

"Whatever it is, you're not about to eat it this late at night at my house. You gon' get me an ass-whoopin from yo mama too. Whatever you about to eat, go put it in the kitchen so that I know you ain't sneaking and eating it. Doug around here somewhere. Go see if you can find him. Play with Doug till yo mama get here."

Olivia had this cat named Doug. I've never been a fan of cats, but I liked Doug. The scent of secondhand smoke was embedded in his fur. He smelled like he hadn't been given a bath in months and limped like he'd never seen a veterinarian. From Doug's body language, you could tell he was never really a fan of kids, but he liked me. It was a mutual toleration.

I placed the Twinkie on the kitchen counter and walked around the house to find Doug. I spotted him under a love seat in the living room.

I gently petted this stinking-ass cat and occasionally would play tug-of-war with him with one of his pet toys. It wasn't much, but it was enough to pass away the time. *Note to self: Next time you run away from home, pack a Voltron Lion.* Ten minutes must've gone by before I heard the low rumble of the doo-doo green Cutlass Supreme approaching.

My mother walked in the door and greeted Olivia, and they proceeded to go into the kitchen and laugh like schoolgirls. My mother shot me a quick look as she passed by me. I wasn't sure if I was in trouble, but even if I was, any fears that I had of my mother were about to be superseded by something far more dangerous. About ten minutes after my mother walked in, the front door swung open again. The person walking in the door this time was taller and heavier. Doug sprung to his feet and disappeared at warp speed under a love seat. I looked up to see Olivia's husband, Keith, towering over me.

Keith was a pretty big dude, well over six feet tall, with muscles coming out of his muscles. He was one of those guys who, no matter what athletic jersey you put him in, looked like he could play that sport. His eyes were cold and black and filled with the regret of a life unfulfilled. He didn't walk through the house, he prowled like a great white shark. You could never be sure if he was just passing by or about to strike. Olivia normally babysat me at my momma's apartment, so it was rare that I ever saw Keith. If I did, he was generally indifferent toward me. We locked eyes for a second and he grimaced. He knew that if I was there, then my mother wasn't that far away.

Keith took off his work vest and lumbered through the living room. The impact of his work boots hitting the floor shook the dirt loose from them, leaving a trail of mess on the smoke-scented carpet. First stop, the kitchen.

Keith joined my mother and Olivia in the kitchen, out of my sight line. In those days, kids weren't allowed to be in the same room with socializing adults. Fine by me, the way I figured it. The longer I stayed out of sight, the more time I had to figure a way out of my current predicament. The lady I was running away from had come to pick me up and take me back home, the exact place I'd just run away from. I didn't want to be here, but I couldn't just sneak out the house because I didn't fucking know the way to anywhere else but school. For the time being, I was stuck.

To buy myself some time, I retreated to the love seat to lure out Doug. But no amount of cooing or meowing could get him out of there. Suddenly the music in the kitchen stopped, and Doug took off like a lightning bolt, this time to the back of the house in the bedrooms. I was alone.

Looking to see where Doug had gone, I heard a scream escape from the kitchen.

"Keith, *no!*"

By the time I turned around to see what was happening, Olivia was already airborne, flying into the living room, both her feet off the ground. She landed on her back and hit her head pretty good on the brick area around their fireplace. Keith came stomping into the living room. Making sure she stayed down, he towered over her. I wanted to check on her, but Keith caught me out the corner of his eye.

Folding his hand into a fist, he'd barely taken half a step toward me before I heard my mother.

"Roy, go put your bike in my car!"

She walked over very calmly and stood between me and Keith. She'd stood up to Jim Crow in Mississippi. This was light work. She didn't yell or make any sudden movements, so as to not set off the grizzly bear we were now face-to-face with. Still, I couldn't move.

"Boy, I said go put your goddamn bike in the goddamn car! *Now!*"

My mother had given me a clear directive, but I wasn't going to leave her. We were going to face this man together. My mother had a younger brother who served in the army. Whenever he came home from deployment, he taught my mother and her sisters some self-defense moves. And I spent most Saturday afternoons watching kung fu movies. I figured that between the two of us, we should be able to land at least one blow.

Keith huffed and puffed and stared my mother down. He didn't blink, and neither did she. His hand slowly relaxed until he was no longer making a fist. A new decision had been made.

Keith turned and slowly lumbered out of the room. He grabbed the TV remote and disappeared into the couch much in the same way Godzilla slowly returns to the ocean, leaving behind nothing but destruction and chaos.

Only Olivia's weeping hung in the air now.

"Get to the car, please," my mother said while rushing to get Olivia some tissue. As I made my way to the door, a different noise filled the air, the crinkling of a Twinkies wrapper. I looked over at the couch and saw that Keith was eating my Twinkie. He looked at me and smiled.

Well, played, motherfucker.

The ride home was quiet. *What could have happened*, I thought to myself, *if my mother hadn't been there to protect me from Keith?* When we got back to the house, I put my bicycle away and then went upstairs, changed back into my pajamas, and lay down. Whatever trouble or discipline or talking-to that I was due for running away had been "waived on account of rain." I knew I wasn't in trouble anymore because my mom came in the room to tuck me in and simply asked, "Are you okay?"

I replied, "I'm sorry for eating the candy. It won't happen again."

"If you had just said that the first time I was up here, we wouldn't have almost had to fight a grizzly bear tonight," she replied. We shared a brief chuckle, and then it was lights out.

That night wouldn't be the last time I disobeyed my mom, but it was the first time I realized that I needed someone. Just because you can slice your own oranges doesn't mean you're ready for the world. Had she not been there, who knows what Keith would've done to me.

I felt an unspeakable level of fear that night—a fear that as a man I would never want to instill into a child. For sure, I can be stern as a dad, but to have your child horrified of you, I'm not sure how any man could ever be okay with that, because there's no coming back from that. There is no rebuilding trust after morphing into such a monster in the eyes of a child.

In under twenty minutes, my mother showed me two things that you need to make it in this world: fire and compassion. I learned a lot of things from the men in this book, but my mother showed me compassion and for that, I'm forever grateful.

I hadn't even given that night with Keith and my mom that much thought until decades later when I was walking the streets of New York City with you, son. I'd had a testy exchange with a man on a subway train and I briefly glimpsed my reflection in the window, with you at my side. I looked just like my mother did that night at Olivia's house. Ready for anything.

CHAPTER 2

The Fire Boat Race of 1985

was probably the only Black child who was happy to see cotton fields. Seeing that ocean of white in the Mississippi Delta as we drove down Highway 61 outside of Memphis was how I knew I was heading south, to my mother's hometown of Clarksdale, Mississippi.

The best days were when the crop dusters would fly alongside the car. On a good day I'd see a tiny plane showing off for traffic below. The pilots would do loops and barrel rolls over the fields as they sprayed insecticides over the crops, and sometimes also over the freeway itself.

Mmmmm, the sweet smell of poison coming through the air con-ditioner vents.

My mother hated the one-hour drive. I saw it in her face. She'd picked cotton in these same fields as a child in the 1950s South. Before her, my grandmother did it. I'm sure the cotton fields repre-sented the life she was trying to escape—the very reason she was busting her ass in grad school in the first place. It's hard to believe that the place you are from has evolved, when the only sign of progress is an airplane flying over your old place of work.

Eager to have some time to herself, my mother would drop me off in Clarksdale one weekend a month and two months in the summer. There, my Grandma Vera and a plethora of relatives were at the ready to step in and watch me. Summertime was especially great because my other cousins from all over the country would also descend upon Clarksdale, so right away I had something there that I lacked in Memphis—community.

Every day in Clarksdale, kids my age littered the streets. Between me and my cousins, there were seven of us, but usually there were about four of us together at any given time. Tasha was our leader. She was only three years older than me, but in the '80s, that basically made her a legal guardian. There were the Walls' kids across the street: Kwami, Kamar, and Joe. The five Frazier kids next door. Fruit, Ed, Gus, and the boys who would come from a few streets over. It was crazy. Counting me, that was enough for six-on-six street football. And if all the kids at the other end of the street came down, we could field a proper nine-on-nine baseball game and have a designated hitter.

There were so many kids in the street every day that we were essentially kidnap-proof. No kidnapping van had that kind of seating capacity. You'd need a fifteen-seater to scoop us up, and even then you'd still leave behind three to four witnesses. This kind of strength in numbers gave adults on the street comfort and left us unsupervised, as long as we stayed on Andrews Street.

If we dared to wander, the adults had spies all over the city who would quickly tell us to get back home before they snitched on us. This was the era when you could get a whooping or get cursed out by a random woman that you didn't know, only to find out on Sunday that she sang in the choir with your aunt.

We played from sunup until sundown, stopping only for ten minutes in the late afternoon when the mosquito truck came through spraying insecticide in the air to treat the insect infestations. We were so anxious to get back to playing that we did not wait the allotted twenty minutes for the insecticide to dissipate. Eventually we just played football in the poison mist.

Mmmmm, the sweet smell of mosquito poison coming through your nose.

Some days, the mosquito man was the first adult we'd see. You could go *hours* without a grown-up barking orders at you.

If we got hungry, no problem: Smaller, more nimble kids like me were deployed to sneak into people's backyards and scale their trees to collect bags of pecans or crab apples. It could land you a solid bag of food or a solid ass whooping. I once stripped 40 percent of the blossoms off a honeysuckle bush in a lady's backyard with the idea that I would use the juice from the honeysuckles to make "Honeysuckle Lemonade."

Four of us got a solid ass-whooping for that one.

If we needed money for real food, we went door to door and offered to do chores. Sometimes we did yardwork; sometimes grown-ups would send us to the corner store for groceries or cigarettes. We'd take the one or two dollars we made from this illegal child labor and ransack Ms. Lena's corner store for candy. No matter who did what job, we always split the candy evenly. You gotta live by a code.

True freedom. We governed ourselves. This was *Lord of the Flies*–type shit.

Mississippi was the first place I'd felt real freedom, and I was hooked.

■ ■ ■

This Mississippi freedom meant that every summer I returned to Memphis a little more resilient and a little more outspoken against my mother's strict after-school policies at home.

Life in Memphis was much more on the straight and narrow.

My best guess is that my mother did not want other parents in the apartment complex to know I was latchkey, so I wasn't given the same range of freedom as I was in Mississippi.

I pressed and pressed the issue, and by second grade I had negotiated to be able to ride my bike up and down my street in the apartment complex (equivalent to about fifty yards of pavement), but I could not leave our street. Compounding the problem was the fact that, unlike Andrews Street in Clarksdale, my street in Memphis did not have any kids on it.

Coventry Creek Apartments was a sprawling maze of streets that ran between townhomes and units across an acre or two of land. Dense forest bordered one side of the complex, and a creek ran through the middle. There was so much to explore. No kid could stay solely on one street.

The older kids in fourth and fifth grades would tease me about the fact that I couldn't leave my own street. They were free. I wasn't. They'd come whizzing around corners on their dirt bikes, poppin' wheelies on the speed bumps. With candy in one hand, some random turtle they found at the creek in the other, they lived like merry men. Meanwhile I rode alone on a single street doing U-turns up and down the block like a goldfish in an aquarium.

One day when I was in third grade my mother finally bent and allowed me to join this pack of wild wolves. I was riding my bike with them, speeding through Coventry Creek, and it felt like I was back in Mississippi. We skipped rocks, we chased the stray dogs, we climbed trees. We were men, at least until when our parents got home and we had to go take a bath.

The biggest difference I observed right away between Memphis and Clarksdale was the age of the kids that were outside. In Mississippi my group of merry men were pretty much all the same age, give or take a year or two. When you're seven, hanging with a nine-year-old isn't that much of a jump. But in Memphis some of the kids were as much as four to five years older than me. That is a huge jump. If you're seven and you're hanging with a twelve-year-old, you might as well be hanging with a grown-ass man who has a full beard, a union job, and an alcohol problem.

Huge difference.

Couple that age gap with the fact that most men want to impress men older than them, regardless of age, and you have a problem. This desire was my biggest downfall.

The other thing I picked up on quickly was that fifth graders aren't only independent, they're also anti-authority. There was a security guard in our apartment complex who would ride around on a golf cart in the late afternoon and question the kids about various acts of vandalism that had occurred.

"Shut yo ass up, motherfucker!" one of the kids snarled at him. The security guard would hurl profanities back at the kids and this became their relationship. It was very Tom and Jerry.

I was standing there with my mouth open because I didn't even know that you could talk to adults like that and not get punched into next week. In Mississippi I could get a whipping just for being on the wrong street, let alone for cursing at someone. It was amazing to witness.

To be a child is to be convinced that no matter what you've learned, you've already learned everything you need to know to proceed in life without your parents. Even if these boys at Coventry Creek didn't know everything, they acted like they did. It's why I looked up to them so much. They behaved as if they knew everything, and if they did not know something, they had the confidence to believe they would figure it out.

The more I hung with fifth graders, the more I noticed that the fifth graders loved to hang with the sixth graders, and a sixth grader is essentially just a kid doing an impersonation of an eighth grader. So now I was basically a third grader who was hanging with a bunch of eighth graders.

What could possibly go wrong?

Another big difference between Mississippi and Memphis was that in Mississippi, most of the kids feared the father or adult they had to answer to. The threat of an occasional ass-whooping or grounding reminded us of the importance of thinking before we acted.

In Memphis, the kids didn't seem to be fearful of their parents or authority in general. We acted first and we thought later.

With grave consequences.

It all started with an oak tree. At least I think it was an oak tree. Either way, the leaves of that tree made for some of the most fun that we had as kids in Coventry Creek.

The creek that ran through the middle of the complex was officially called Dove Creek, but we called it Coventry Creek. It was barely wide enough to even be called a creek, probably closer to a babbling brook. It was just deep enough for a few fish and crawdads to live in, but it was still narrow enough in places for a squirrel to hop across in a single leap. After a good day of thunderstorms, though, the rainwater runoff would transform Coventry Creek into a fast-moving body of water. A creek that had barely come up to your shoelaces before now reached the middle of your thigh.

Rain was a welcome treat because it meant that for the next few days the creek would be deep enough for us to have what we called "leaf races."

The leaf of the southern wild oak is very thick and about six inches long, and we chose it for our races because it curved upward in the front and back like the bow and stern of a boat. A sturdy vein ran down the center and operated as a boat keel. The leaf's slick surface also proved to be very waterproof.

We'd gather at an overpass in the middle of the complex that stood over the creek. I'd stand shoulder to shoulder with all the other kids, and we'd drop our leaves at the same time. The leaves flipped and fluttered in the air in a race to get to the water. Once on the water, the leaves would dip and move with the water current and race downstream to a predetermined finish line about twenty yards away.

We usually bet twenty-five cents or a piece of candy on a race.

The fifth graders we used to look up to were now seventh graders, and they didn't have time to hang with us anymore. They'd discovered more important things like girls, erections, and videogames. Without the guidance of our immature drill sergeants, we were free to make dumb decisions on our own. The decision we made on this day involved a lighter and pine needles.

Highly *flammable* pine needles.

We had an idea: Instead of having just a leaf go down the water, how cool would it be if there was a pile of pine needles on fire on top of the leaf as it made its way down the stream? A fire boat race!

Like the perfectly reasonable group of grown men that we were, we all agreed this was a brilliant idea. We combed the bank of the creek for dry pine needles until we each held a tight bundle in our hands.

Each competitor would place his leaf in the water, holding it by the stem while another person loaded pine needles into the cargo area. A third party would then set those pine needles on fire, and the competitors would release their fire boats downstream at the same time like a Viking funeral.

We did this about three or four times with no real problems. Then someone saw smoke.

"Oh shit! What's that down there?" one of the kids mumbled. We noticed that about fifteen yards downstream, one of the fire boats had gotten caught in a side current and reached the side of the riverbank, where there were dried leaves and pine needles.

Further compounding the problem, the fire was on the far side of the creek. And there was just enough water in the creek that I couldn't hopscotch across on the rocks without getting my feet wet.

"Somebody gotta go put that out."

"Well, it's not gonna be me."

"Well, it's not going to be me either."

"It should be you."

"I ain't crossing that creek."

"These my only shoes for school. I can't get them wet."

"Somebody should take off their shoes, then you won't get them wet."

"But those rocks will cut your feet."

"Those rocks aren't going to cut your feet."

"Well, since the rocks don't cut feet, then you should go."

"I'm not going."

As we bickered, the small plumes of smoke slowly grew into rolling flames. It was now a fire we were no longer qualified to extinguish.

As the fire spread, we casually debated telling the security guard. Instead of bothering that kind gentleman with our tribulations, we all hopped on our bikes and sped home. We all agreed to stay inside for the rest of the day and not come back out.

You know how arsonists always return to the scene of the crime in movies? I always understood that. I think it's about being in awe that something as small as a spark can grow into something so massive and destructive.

As I sat at home watching Nickelodeon, I could faintly hear the siren of a fire engine in the distance, then another, and then another. I waited about an hour, the curiosity was killing me. I hopped on my bike and slowly returned to the scene of the crime. There were three fire trucks there. Smoke filled the air, and there were so many fire hoses on the ground it made more sense to walk my bike than attempt to hop over them. The fire had spread across the embankment and up a telephone pole. As I scanned the scene, I realized that the security guard was there watching the crowd as well. He and I locked eyes. He just knew I was involved. I don't know how, but he *knew*. I hopped on my chariot and pedaled away.

"Hey! Come here!" he yelled as I sped away. "Come here! Come here! You little motherfucka!"

I got away. The next afternoon I told the crew what happened. We held a meeting and figured it would be best if we all stayed inside and lay low, figuring the security guard wouldn't see us and would just forget we were suspects.

He didn't forget.

That night, my mom came in the house late as usual and as was tradition when matters were pressing, she woke me up out of my sleep. This time, though, it wasn't shock and awe. She said in an oddly calm tone, "They saying some of the kids 'round here started that fire the other day. Were you outside that day?"

"No, ma'am, I was home."

"Roy, you do know if they can prove that you were there when that fire started, they could evict us?" She never raised her voice, but she also never made eye contact. I said nothing. I wasn't going to snitch on my guys.

"Okay. Have a good evening," she said. When she got to the door, she turned and said, "I noticed a pair of your shoes were soaking wet."

She closed the door and left.

The conversation was never about the fire. It was about me lying to her, and I believe that my lying confirmed to her that she'd lost control of me. Without a father around, it's very easy to see how young kids can become influenced by the streets. I had a crew. I belonged and I wasn't going to be a tattletale.

I got shipped off to Mississippi that summer, same as always, but when it was time to go back to Memphis, I noticed immediately the lack of cotton fields. Then I noticed that we were on Highway 78 and not Highway 61.

"Where are we going?" I asked.

"Birmingham," she replied. "We are moving to Birmingham to live with your father. I've already packed up your things."

My mother had never told me we were going to Birmingham. I literally found out when we were already in the car and halfway there. I went ballistic. I cried the two and a half hours from Clarksdale to Tupelo. Mischievous as they were, my Memphis friends were still my friends, and I wasn't even given the dignity of being able to tell them goodbye.

But can you blame my mother? Considering what I had pulled in running away to Olivia's house, what I had pulled at Southland Mall, and what I had now pulled in blatantly lying to her about the fire, I don't think my mother had any choice but to keep the move a secret. There's no telling how I would have reacted. Up until that point, all the men in my life had taught me was how to punch a woman in the face and burn down an apartment complex.

But now she knew, if nothing else, I would be closer to my father and have a live-in enforcer. As we passed through Tupelo, my crying subsided. We spent the last two hours of the ride in silence, not knowing what this move to Birmingham would mean for either of us.

Just before the Alabama state line, my mother stopped for gas. She went inside to pay and bought a few snacks. When she got back to the car, she pulled two hot dogs out of the bag and handed them to me.

"Unwrap my hot dog and give it to me with a few napkins," she mumbled.

We were still a team.

She put the car in drive and the 1975 doo-doo green Cutlass Supreme crept back onto Highway 78, taking us to a place we knew would change us forever. It just remained to be seen how.

CHAPTER 3

Welcome to Birmingham

Before my mom and I moved to Birmingham, my interactions with my dad were only once a month and we had very little contact outside of those visits. I'm not sure it's fair to say that my father had *no* interest in my life in the Memphis years—beyond being a disciplinarian—but I sometimes wish that he'd taken me out for ice cream when he'd visited, rather than just scolding me and sending me to bed. Sometimes he would pull up with a toy or take me to McDonald's, but more often than not, if he came to town and I was already in the doghouse, he'd exact his usual form of punishment. Because he was disappointed and uptight with me, we would not get to spend much time together.

In those Memphis days, fear was the language my father and I spoke. And I soon became fluent. I can recall more times I was afraid of my dad than times when I felt generally loved. If we spoke by phone, it was usually to correct me or reprimand me. We did not have many run-of-the-mill "How was your day?" conversations. Put a gun to his head and I don't think he could have told you my favorite cartoon or favorite food. But I knew to say "Yes, sir," and "No, sir." He commanded respect and demanded it of me often.

I don't even think my father was capable of "How was your day?" conversation. He was sixty-three when I was born in 1978, so maybe at his age he was just tired of small talk. He'd heard it all before. I am my mother's only child, but I am the ninth of his eleven children. If nothing else, my father could charm many a woman into a bed. But men of his age—particularly Black men—had also been hardened by life. I can only imagine the traumas he carried. When he was four years old, his own father just "disappeared" in the middle of the night in his hometown of Atlanta. Since it was the South in the 1920s, one can only assume that my grandfather not returning home to be with my father was because he'd been murdered. The body of my grandfather was never found, and his disappearance remains a mystery to this day. After that, my father and his mother, like many other Black people in the South, migrated north to Chicago. His mother never remarried, and there was never another male head of household in his home.

My father's pain wasn't just psychological. At age thirteen, he'd been the victim of a horrible car accident that shattered his hip so terribly he was given a prosthetic hip. As he grew, he had to receive repeated hip transplants so that the bone could be extended to keep up with puberty. Even with the best medical technology available at that time, one of my father's legs remained shorter than the other, and he had to wear an elevated shoe and walk with a limp. And if that's not bad enough, he was growing up physically disabled, without a father, in a rough part of Chicago, in the middle of Jim Crow segregation.

As a teenager, his depression forced his mother to send him to a psychiatrist. It was the psychiatrist who complimented his voice and suggested he go into radio. So he did just that.

My father used the bass from his window-rattling voice to build a name for himself in radio news. His voice was so smooth and so perfect, many news directors did not know he was Black. My father would hop off the train somewhere in the Midwest and head to a radio station for his job interview only to be greeted by gasps and pearl-clutching by people in the radio station. But my dad was so smooth he could charm the prejudice off of a white man faster than he could the panties of the women he dated. At many places he worked in the 1940s and 1950s, my father was the first Black employee. He took a liking to covering civil rights. It made sense considering racism had taken his father from him.

Global conflicts that most reporters ran from, my father ran to. He took sniper fire in the then African nation of Rhodesia during a civil war that would eventually birth the nation of Zimbabwe. On that same continent he would take sniper fire in Soweto as he covered an uprising in South Africa. During the Vietnam War he volunteered to be embedded with Black troops from the Chicago area to get firsthand accounts of their experiences during the war so that he could air those interviews on his home station in Chicago, WVON, the Voice of the Negro. And let's not forget the good old-fashioned domestic American racism he'd experienced covering the civil rights movement and every horror that spanned it. Name a riot from that era and my father covered it—Watts in '65, Detroit in '67, Newark, Harlem, the riots of '68 after Dr. Martin Luther King Jr. was assassinated.

Something that we may consider commonplace today my father launched during this same time in Chicago at WVON. He and a few other people cofounded what would come to be known as the National Black Network. NBN was the first coast-to-coast radio network fully owned by African Americans. There were a number of news updates and sports scores interspersed with community affairs and news programs. My father was the news director and quarterback of a syndicated talk and call-in show, *One Black Man's Opinion.*

My father also found time to mentor a young Chicago police

officer who was looking to quit the force and get into media. His name was Don Cornelius. My father was one of the handful of people who loaned Don some of the money to shoot the pilot for what would eventually become the empire that he created for himself, *Soul Train*. Much like the guy who divested from Facebook in the early days or the dude that left Apple before Steve Jobs took it to the top, my dad got his money back from Don and wanted no parts of a singing and dancing show. I guess it's kind of hard to sit and watch Black people dance and be happy when you have spent almost four decades seeing them suffer.

After Chicago he eventually ended up in New York City for CBS Radio before finally taking the job as news director of the Black-owned radio station WENN 107.7. There he curated a great deal of media and talk show content similar to the programming that was carried on NBN. Birmingham would be his last stop professionally.

My point is, my father had a front row seat to some of the worst things the world had to offer, so you probably don't want to have a chuckle with an eight-year-old child about his Voltron Black Lion. (My mother eventually got me one.)

The prospect of living with my father full-time was a little nerve-racking because my short visits to Birmingham—usually the first month of my summer vacations—had always been like a splash of cold water. My father wasn't a fan of my mother's latchkey parenting strategy. As much as my mother trusted me to do the right thing and stay in the house, he never believed I would honor such a pact in Birmingham when there was so much new undiscovered country to explore in his neighborhood. So I spent most of my time *with* my dad. I was his shadow. Wherever he went, I went, starting with his job at the radio station at 5:30 *in the fucking morning*, where, shockingly, there were no kids to play with.

We'd pick up Hardee's and a newspaper on the way to the radio station, and as he read the news of the day to the world, I would sit on the floor at his feet quietly eating a sausage biscuit. I couldn't crinkle the wrapper too loud while he was on the air or that newspaper he just bought would get rolled very tight into a weapon and I'd get popped in the mouth for making noise over a live microphone. It was a quick open-handed strike—silent, yet stinging, far too soft to be a slap by definition but definitely hard enough to stun you and knock the Hardee's biscuit out your mouth.

This would go on over the next two hours until around 7:30 in the morning, when he'd pass me off to his friend Frankie Palmer for what was his version of affordable babysitting. I don't remember what Ms. Palmer did for a living, but her side job was to pick me up from the radio station in the morning and drop me off at Kingston Elementary School on the north side of town. As it turned out, Memphis schools ended before Birmingham schools, so my father's idea of a fun summer vacation from school was to send me back to school.

Every day, Ms. Palmer would walk me into Kingston, where she'd pass me off to a school official who knew which classroom to take me to. It's crazy to think about that now, but that's how much respect my father commanded in the Black community. In a city like Birmingham that is around 75 percent Black, my father was on the radio every morning. He had as much power as the mayor. He literally could call a school principal and basically say, "Hey, my son is in town. I'm too cheap to hire a babysitter. Stick him in the back of somebody's classroom and teach him some shit."

Whatever grade I was headed to in Memphis was the classroom my father would stick me in. The summer I graduated kindergarten, my reward was to sit in on the last two weeks of first grade. He saw it as an opportunity to give me a sneak preview of whatever lesson I'd be learning the next year.

The school asked for no enrollment paperwork, no immunization forms, no verification of address, just an off-the-cuff request for an unsanctioned education for the child of the most popular and most respected Black radio newsman in town. Not only did they not ask questions, school officials were honored my father even chose their school to shadily educate his child. In a day and age where most people use their celebrity for free sneakers and courtside seats, it's kind of wild to think that a man could just call and demand that his child sit in a public school classroom while he worked or ran errands.

As far as my father was concerned, school was the best form of childcare. I wasn't crazy about the arrangement, but it was better than being at the radio station all day. I was essentially back in school, but it did not matter whether I made good grades. If Ms. Palmer drove fast enough, I could sneak into the cafeteria and wolf down a second breakfast before the first bell. The rest of the day was just me looking forward to lunch and PE.

If I found myself in Birmingham after their school system had let out, my father's alternative to sending me to school was to enroll me in the downtown YMCA and later the Boys and Girls Club of Alabama. It was simple: he dropped me off at 9:00 in the morning and picked me up at 4:00 P.M. Fatherhood was a piece of cake.

But school wasn't just about childcare to my father. He was so serious about education that I don't recall talking to him about much else. All he cared about was learning and discipline. Everyone had a job to do, and to him you were either doing your job or you weren't.

"You'll always be worth more from your neck up than you will ever be from your neck down," he'd say sternly. Any moment he had, my father took the opportunity to remind me about the importance of getting an education. I'm sure the accident he'd had as a child that shattered his thigh had a lot to do with how he viewed physicality as a fickle tool for profit.

Spending my days at Kingston Elementary School was a bit scary at first simply because I was the new guy. But for whatever reason, kids didn't bother me. None of them tried to be my friend but none of them bullied me, which was perfect to me. One of the kids thought that I had been suspended all year and was just now being allowed back in class. That rumor began to spread and by lunch I was someone to avoid. I was able to walk tall on that fable for a couple of days. "What he do that got him suspended in August and *just now* allowed back in school in May?" the other kids would whisper before eventually finding out that I was the child of the dude on the radio.

But that's how admired my father was. His news commentary on the Black struggle and his ability to use his show *One Black Man's Opinion* to illuminate Black issues and have conversations with prominent voices in the Black community had made him a household name in Birmingham long before he moved there.

His voice was so bombastic that it felt like you were listening to a Southern Baptist preacher. Some people even addressed my father as "Reverend Wood." That always made me laugh because if those people knew my father, they would know that the last place he would want to be was inside a church unless they were giving him money to speak there—which ironically was how he spent most of his weekends.

Churches and colleges would hire my father to speak at their events. He would show up and deliver a bombastic message of Black righteousness, take home a nice check, and shake a few hands, then we would be on our way in his Lincoln Continental. I didn't realize it at the time, but the seeds of performance in my own life were being sown.

I enjoyed those trips with my father. If breakfast was when I felt closest to my mother, travel was the only time I felt close to him— like I was getting an opportunity to learn who he was and what made him tick. Travel was also the only time that I had my father to myself. In every other scenario, someone was in his face. He was either handling business or shaking hands with people in the community. He was a star, but worse, he was respected.

There wasn't a place we went in Birmingham where someone

did not want to speak to my father. And he loved conversation with strangers. Radio and television have a way of forging a powerful relationship with a listener. They teach you that in journalism school—in radio you have an audience of one. So when people see you out and about, they already feel like they know you. Couple that with my father's charisma and charm, and it was easy to see why he was the man everyone wanted to have a drink with and every woman wanted to lie with.

My father would scoop me up after work and I would run errands with him the rest of the day. He never treated my visiting him as an opportunity to do anything special together. In a lot of ways I just merged into my father's life and tagged along with him as he went about his day. I did everything with him, be it car repairs or grocery shopping or a trip to a local pawnshop, camera shop, or flea market. My dad loved photography and was always looking to track down the latest in camera lenses and recording equipment. He was an avid collector of old cameras: Canons, Nikons, or the old-school Ricohs. My father would spend Sunday morning reading the classified ads in the newspaper and circling leads, and we would spend the back half of the day on Sunday following up on all of those leads.

The summers in Birmingham every year gave me some sense of familiarity with the community at large, so when my mother and I got there in 1985 it wasn't exactly a foreign place to me. But that didn't mean it was easy.

■ ■ ■

The first thing I noticed when I moved into my father's house was that there wasn't much to do in the house, and the neighborhood wasn't nearly as inviting as Coventry Creek.

Not only could I no longer play on my entire street, I could only play in my yard. It turned out that the movers my mom hired were shady. They stole practically everything from the truck, including my bicycle.

My father lived in a towering two-story, four-bedroom house in the Birmingham neighborhood of West End. In the 1980s West End was predominantly Black thanks in part to the white flight exodus of white residents to the suburbs, but there were still a few pockets of white people, mostly the ones who couldn't afford the "flight" part of "white flight." The white people who couldn't afford the migration to the suburbs and remained in West End were all very resilient in their own way.

About six doors down from my father's house was a clubhouse/bar for an all-white motorcycle gang. They rode through West End cranking their bikes very loudly, I guess to intimidate Black people in the neighborhood or to just peacock and make their presence known. They never smiled; they never waved; and if you ever made eye contact with one of them, they'd give you the middle finger.

White people who remained in Black neighborhoods during white flight weren't to be fucked with, they were the toughest of the toughest. Some were even members of the Black street gang Gangster Disciples that reigned supreme in West End at the time. We called them GDs.

Two doors over from my father was an active crack house. I know this because the sweet old white lady Mrs. Murray who lived between us and the crack house told us so. The crack house thankfully was the type of spot that just dealt the drugs. No one stayed there and did the drugs. As far as crack houses go, this was a best-case scenario.

Carry-out only. No dine-in.

All of this was within two blocks of my father's home: a biker gang, a crack house, a liquor store, Gangster Disciples patrolling the streets, and a Seventh-Day Adventist church. At night, the sounds of passing freight trains filled the air in between the distant gunshots. In the rare moments of quiet, you could hear the walls in the house creaking and shifting and popping. It was scary.

West End was also overrun with stray dogs that were very aggressive. They had claimed my father's driveway and backyard as their territory, so me being there playing catch with myself with a tennis ball against the side of the garage was viewed as an act of war. For every child in the neighborhood there were at least four stray dogs. And these were not the kind of dogs that you would chase for fun, these dogs chased *you*.

I generally was never outside more than ten minutes before being run inside for thirty minutes because one of the dogs wanted to come and take a shit in the yard. So I did not have a lot of time to work on my baseball fielding skills.

Inside the house, I didn't have many freedoms either. My father had only one television with a cable connection, and he made it perfectly clear that it was *his* television, and he oversaw what he was going to watch. Back in Memphis, my mother was always gone so I had the freedom to watch whatever I wanted to watch. Though I mostly picked the same shows, I primarily only watched PBS and Nickelodeon. I watched *Reading Rainbow, Wild America, You Can't Do That on Television, Danger Mouse,* and *Double Dare*. Once we got to Birmingham, all that stopped. I don't think I ever watched a second of Nickelodeon again after we moved to Birmingham.

At the time, my mother never explicitly stated to me why we were moving to Birmingham, but I knew deep down it was so my dad could be in my life. It was clear to me from week one of our arrival that she was not going to benefit from this personally that much. The irony about my mom moving to Birmingham so that I could be closer to my father was that he worked so much that I saw him about the same amount of time as I had when we lived in Memphis. Clearly, our presence wasn't going to force him to deviate from his life already in progress.

It wasn't so much that my parents got back together as that my mother and I moved in with my father. My father was in a relationship with a woman across town and they had just welcomed their second child. My father often spent most of his nights at her house. If this arrangement presented complexities for my mother, I think it was offset by the comfort of knowing that if I got into any mischief, I still would have to immediately answer to a man who would not hesitate to impose his will and slap the biscuit out my mouth. There would be no "leaf races" in Birmingham.

The funny thing is that I didn't even know that my parents were separated. My mother never sat me down and gave me that corny family sitcom bullshit: "Okay, son, sometimes people still love each other but don't live together and blah blah blah." But when your father takes you over to his girlfriend's house so you can meet your two brothers, you kinda figure out that your dad and your mom have much different dynamics going on than in a typical home. I'd watched enough episodes of *The Cosby Show* and *Family Matters* to know my home structure wasn't normal.

Still, none of this seemed weird to me because I started out without my father in my home. The household of my mother and me was the baseline. My father was the equivalent of the character that is added to your favorite television show somewhere in the middle of its run. I had friends who grew up with two parents and I also had friends who were raised by single moms. Some were being physically abused by their mother's boyfriends, and some were being physically abused by their mothers. I felt lucky in comparison.

My father was a creature of habit. In the afternoons, he watched the usual afternoon talk/news magazine shows until the local news came on at 5:00 P.M. He watched the local news on NBC at 5:00, then at 5:30 the local news on ABC, and then at 6:00 the local news on CBS. Some nights he would even flip between all three local news channels at the same time, to see the order in which they aired stories. Six-thirty was usually *Wheel of Fortune* or *Jeopardy!*

At 7:00 P.M. he switched over to C-SPAN before switching over to CNN to take in national news and *Larry King Live*. Sometimes he put a tape recorder beside the television to record sound bites if there was an interesting guest and he wanted to play audio from that guest during his news clips the next morning. He concluded the evening with the local news at 10 P.M. and headed to bed. The only time he made a departure from this routine was during Black History Month when PBS would air the miniseries *Roots* over the course of ten nights in prime time. My father never watched TV to be entertained. It was a vessel of information. I never saw him watch a scripted drama. I never saw him watch a sitcom. Jazz music was his only other escape.

Rather than watch the black-and-white TV that was in my room, I sat in the living room and watched these programs with him. This was where my consumption of news and information began. We did not talk much; we just watched the news and during commercial breaks discussed the stories. If I ever asked a question, he was happy to answer. But for the most part I was content just watching whatever he was watching.

But as much as my father wanted me to live a life of constant supervision, he had to concede some afternoons and evenings because he had places to be. He couldn't tuck me away in elementary school all summer, so rather than leave me home alone, he opted to enroll me in the Boys and Girls Club down the street from the house. My mother had secured a job at the University of Alabama at Birmingham, so on her way to work she would drop me off at the local Boys Club. I would stay there until 5:00 P.M. and then walk myself back home.

I had a good time at the Boys Club, but in my opinion it was just a nice minimum-security prison. It was isolated like one. The facility was surrounded by thick forest on most sides and nestled in the heart of West End at the end of a long industrial road. You could sneak out, but it would be at least a twenty-minute walk immersed in that July Alabama heat before you hit a main road. You're better off staying inside. There was plenty to do—swimming pools, basketball, flag football, videogames, bumper pool—and I made a few friends. There was even a decent snack booth inside where you could buy candy and treats, so like prison, if you had the money then you could purchase amenities for yourself to make your stay more comfortable, but you weren't allowed to leave the property.

Whatever sense of independence I had been given in Memphis and Clarksdale had been stripped from me when I got to Birmingham. I was still a dog, just on a shorter leash.

■ ■ ■

As summer ended and we got into the school year, my mother and I fell into a pretty regular routine. It wasn't uncommon for my father to disappear for two or three days in a row. I just assumed he was across town with his other family.

In my father's house, one of the hardest things to get used to was the sounds. Neither the kitchen nor the dining room nor the stairs had carpet, and with nothing to absorb the sound, you could hear everything that was happening downstairs all the way upstairs. There was a small desk outside the kitchen that sat near the foot of the stairs. Whatever conversation was happening at that desk, the acoustics of the house carried that sound straight up the stairway into my room.

My mom would come in the house and make a phone call or two, but these calls weren't like the ones she'd made in Memphis. There was no more joy in her voice. Simply by listening to her side of the conversation, I could put together what was happening.

"Hey girl, it's Joyce. . . . Mmm hmmm, everything is fine, how are you? . . . Uh huh. . . . Yep. . . . Look, I wouldn't call you if I didn't need it but I'm having car trouble. . . . The mechanics say it's gonna be five hundred dollars. . . . No, he won't give me the money. He said that giving me a roof was more than enough and I should have it. . . . Uh huh. Girl, thank you. Thank you so much."

The biggest difference from Memphis was that my mother's new job paid less. The little bit of money she had left she was saving to start law school. My mother has a lot of pride, and nothing makes her happier than not asking someone for anything. So, for her to humble herself and ask someone for something—I know that it did something to her.

The one time she cracked was after my yearlong insistence that she let me go to Space Camp in Huntsville. It was the '80s and this movie *Space Camp* had come out. The plot to the movie was fucking ridiculous, but I loved it. A bunch of kids who were in Space Camp pretending to be astronauts somehow ended up in actual fucking space and had to do actual astronaut-type shit to help save the mission and land the shuttle safely. The entire movie was just one big advertisement for NASA, the space program, and Space Camp.

From time to time I would leave the Space Camp brochures in strategic locations around the house. I don't remember what the exact cost was back then, but it was for sure around $1,000 a week. And it was a two-week course.

I was in the fourth grade at this point, so I had a more tactical approach to manipulating my mother. Gone were the days of shock and awe at Southland Mall. I thought that I could win my mother over with the power of persuasion. After months of not mentioning seeing the brochures, I finally flat-out asked her one day if she had looked at the brochure, and she snapped at me.

"I don't have the money, and I don't know when I'm going to get the money," she huffed. "And even when I get the money, I'm not sure if that's what we need to be spending money on." Then she stormed out the room.

I was too young and naive to recognize how much pressure I was putting on my mom by asking for something that she so desperately wanted to provide for me but knew deep down she couldn't.

My persistence forced her to do something she had always avoided doing with me, which was telling me the truth: that she couldn't afford something. She hated to admit that, and anyone or anything that forced that truth out of her mouth she was liable to resent. But shit, man, how was I supposed to know that she didn't have $1,000? My mother had always worked miracles before, so I figured she would be able to work this one too.

I hated myself for making her snap at me. I didn't mean to make her sad. It was the last time I asked my mother for anything that wasn't school related.

I never knew how my parents budgeted their money. I just knew I hated being a burden. Public schools have a way of always springing random charges on parents, and they always come between paychecks. Your kid could come home and need forty dollars for a field trip, and if there's a field trip, that means that they have to eat lunch, which means you have to spring for more than the usual two dollars that it costs for school lunch. Don't forget school picture day; that's another seventy dollars. Or it's fifteen dollars for PE uniforms, or the baseball team is traveling to some Little League tournament so that's one hundred dollars for these little knickknack charges. Every time I went to my mother and asked for money, a look of frustration would come over her face and she would calmly say, "Have you asked your father?"

To which I always wanted to reply, "No, motherfucker, I didn't ask him for the same reason *you* didn't ask him for that car repair money. He won't give you money to go get your car fixed so you can go to work and school and make more money. You really think he's going to give me spending money to buy something from the gift shop at a science museum?"

But instead, I would hold my head low and say, "No, ma'am, I came to you first."

"Well, go to your daddy first, that's part of why he's here," she softly replied.

There was zero chance my pops was going to fund my dreams of going to space. Hell, my father would say no, just for practice. I truly believe he woke up and practiced saying no the way Broadway singers work on their runs before a major performance.

"No. Nooooo! No No No Noooooooooooooo. Nah, Never, Nah, no, neverrrrrrr."

He always thought that food was too expensive. He was a *religious* coupon clipper and would often travel all over the city for different items based on what their prices were in the newspaper. A normal person would have twenty items on the grocery list and maybe split that between two stores. You could give my father that same twenty-item grocery list and he would go to six different stores if he could verify that each store had an item on the list for the cheapest.

He never calculated time and gas spent to save money. For him it was always about getting over on white corporations that he believed charged more for certain items in Black neighborhoods. If he could travel to a white side of town and get that item for cheaper, then he was winning the war on racism.

When I left fifth grade and headed to middle school in the sixth grade, he lost it when he found out that the cost of a school lunch shot up fifty cents from $1.25 to $1.75. It might as well have been $40,000 to my dad. He was so sure I was lying about the price increase he went to the school to verify the price. Then he stayed and demanded to talk to the principal about it. That poor school principal is at her desk trying to solve bigger problems like improving teacher morale and keeping guns out of the schools and here comes her assistant knocking at her door.

"Sorry to bother you, ma'am, but one of the most respected minds in journalism is out here and he wants to know why the rectangle cheese pizzas cost more money in sixth grade than they do in fifth grade considering the pizzas are exactly the same size and come from the same food distributor."

The principal nervously told my father the price increase helped to subsidize the free lunch program because middle school kids were more prone to take advantage of both the free breakfast and the free lunch than the elementary kids. She also said that middle school lunches had larger portion sizes because the kids were hitting puberty. To this day I don't know if that is true, but if it isn't, it is one of the most beautifully delivered pieces of bullshit I've ever heard one adult tell another. My father huffed and conceded the point. As much as he hated how much it cost for school lunch, he knew that if I packed my own lunch it just meant he would have to buy more groceries, which he also hated.

My father *hated* giving up money. When I used to spend the summers with him riding around to the camera shops, he always wanted a cheaper price. He loved to haggle.

I dreaded class field trips. "Boy, why do you need money for McDonald's *and* a souvenir picture? A picture is free!" he'd say. "Go in there and get one of my cameras!"

To my father there would be nothing unusual about a fifth grader showing up to a class field trip, pulling out a Vietnam War–era Ricoh camera and asking everyone to remain still for thirty seconds while the picture took. Yup. Perfectly normal. Even if my father did concede that I deserved to eat at McDonald's, he would never agree to give me the full ten dollars for it.

"A hamburger combo meal is four twenty-three after tax. If I give you six dollars you might can throw in an ice cream cone," he'd say.

I would walk into a McDonald's with my classmates and watch them order the biggest, juiciest burgers, with a large Hi-C orange. I had to pretend that I enjoyed my dry-ass hamburger and a cup of water just so I could afford a caramel sundae at the end of my meal. I guess six dollars is better than nothing. Some days my mom would help negotiate me getting the full ten dollars. On those days, I still skimped when I ate on the field trip and saved my change from that meal to put toward having a bigger lunch at school the following day or gas station candy.

And if the field trip was out of state, he even knew how to compensate for the various state taxes in Georgia and Tennessee. He often drove an hour to the state line just to purchase alcohol for less.

My thirst for money started long before I was at the legal age to work in the state of Alabama, which was fifteen, or fourteen in some cases, depending on the job. I read the newspaper a lot growing up, and from browsing the want ads I learned that people would buy damn near anything. Folks would advertise their yard sales, so every few months or so, even as young as fifth grade, I would have one. When I was done playing with a toy or I felt it had run its course, I would set it out to pasture for one to five dollars. I'd set up the table in the front yard, put out a sign, and sit there and wait for the Saturday yard sale scavengers to drive by.

On a good day I probably would pull in about twenty dollars, not nearly enough for a decent pair of sneakers, but enough to buy souvenirs for the upcoming field trip or to impress whatever girl I had a crush on at school by splurging and getting her an ice cream sandwich at lunch. You know, baller shit.

In middle school, if I was really in a pinch for money, I would sell my Nintendo cartridges. This used to infuriate my mother, so I usually would wait to set up the yard sale until later in the day when she was gone. Once my mother bought me a Nintendo game it disappeared into my room, never to be seen again as far as she was concerned. My mother worked so hard at getting me these things. I believe that it pained her to see me giving up something that she knew brought me so much happiness, and also to see me sell something that she for sure had gotten into a fistfight over on Black Friday.

What she failed to realize is that after you beat a videogame, it's kind of boring to play. Unless you had secret codes to play the game in an altered state, hoarding Nintendo games that I'd already defeated seemed silly to me. Also, most games had sequels, so I would sell the previous title. If I had *Super Mario 3*, I didn't need *Super Mario 2*.

My father loved to see me holding yard sales. He probably figured it was that much less money he had to give me, but he also respected me for it. I think he related to having to make the tough call to get rid of something you love because you really need the money.

He'd come out to the table and ask me how many people had stopped by, what they were asking for, and what they were into. Sometimes he would bring out some of his old camera equipment that he no longer wanted and would add it to the table, hoping a passerby needed a camera that was used to capture pictures from various riots in our nation's history. When I think about it now a lot of the cameras that I sold at that table should have been in a museum with my father's picture next to them.

The downside to my dad seeing me sell stuff at a yard sale was that he believed I made hundreds of dollars. Three hours in the Alabama heat on a good day might yield me forty dollars. In my father's mind, that might as well have been forty thousand. Anytime I asked him for money during that school year, his first retort was "What happened to all the money you made at the yard sale?"

"You mean the yard sale from *four* fucking months ago?"

I'm not sure how much my father thought I was making from selling GI Joes, Transformers, and beat-up Nintendo cartridges, but I assure you it was not enough to make it rain in the gift shop of some science museum.

I was always very good at finding an extra dollar from a side hustle. I don't have a lot of gifts, but sitting still for a day and figuring out how to make money is one of them. While my parents did not believe in paying for chores, thankfully some of the people in the neighborhood did.

The house was encircled by eight oak trees that were forty to fifty feet tall. When fall came, there were so many leaves on the ground that you'd slip and fall. I came to hate October and

November because it meant raking and bagging leaves endlessly. The entire process took about three hours, but as it got colder into November it took four hours once you added in the warming breaks. The frozen hands were actually a benefit because then I couldn't feel the blisters that would form on my thumb from the rake constantly rubbing against them.

One day I was in the front yard raking as usual when a stranger rolled up with a proposition. I don't remember the car exactly. Maybe a Buick or a Cutlass, but it was for sure one of those cars driven by someone who goes to church far too often and drives far too slow in the far-left lane. The window rolled down, revealing a sweet Black lady in her early sixties.

"Young man, I take this road every day. And every few weeks I see you out here raking this person's yard and it always looks so nice when you're done. I think I want to hire you to come do my yard as well. How about I pay you ten dollars and when you're done here, come to my house and rake my front yard."

Then she pulled out a crispy Andrew Jackson and gently laid that twenty-dollar bill in my hand. I was *ecstatic*. Yes! Yes, ma'am, I'll be right there. "Don't get too excited, little boy, I want my ten-dollars' change," she snapped.

Her yard was much smaller, with fewer leaves. Raking leaves in my yard was the equivalent to wearing a weighted vest. So I tore through her yard in under an hour. Bagging the leaves took longer than raking them. No one on the west side of Birmingham was faster.

"Wow, that was really fast. You're pretty good," she said. The woman slowly extended her hand for her ten-dollars' change, but I quickly brokered a deal—"Since I'm so good, how about you let me keep fifteen dollars of your money and I will throw in the backyard as well."

She pondered it for a second then nodded in agreement.

I asked her if there were any other people in the neighborhood who she thought could use the services of my "company." She gave me a few names, and I set off door to door as the newest leaf raker in West End.

Raking leaves was the perfect hustle because I didn't have a lot of competition. In the spring and summer everyone my age cut grass or trimmed hedges. In the fall and winter months most of my competition played football, so they weren't free most of leaf season. They were held hostage at football practice until late into the night, and on Saturdays they had their games.

On a good day after school, I rushed to finish my homework and still have enough time afterward to maybe cram in a yard or two or some door-knocking before dark. Soon I had regular clientele. I would charge ten dollars for the front yard and fifteen dollars for front and back yards. I even finally figured out the concept of layering my clothing so that I wasn't shivering as much. I took some of the money I made and invested in a better rake and some work gloves, which helped to speed along the process.

On a good week I was pulling in anywhere from forty to sixty dollars raking leaves and my parents knew nothing about it. It was going so well that I even forgot to ask my father for lunch money every now and then. I had to remind myself to ask him for extra money here and there just to keep up the façade of being broke. I didn't want them getting suspicious. Pretending I didn't have money was the best way to hide that I did.

I remember having to ask him for money for a field trip one time and him going on and on about how I didn't need money for souvenirs or for riding any of the extra rides at the museum. He gave me enough money for the usual McDonald's hamburger combo. I held my head low and pretended to be sad as usual. I walked out of the house that morning for that field trip with eighty dollars in my pocket. If you show up for a school field trip with eighty dollars in your pocket, you might as well show up with forty thousand.

If you ask me to tell you what I bought on these field trips, I really don't remember, but one thing I distinctly remember was a trip to McDonald's when I had *two* meals. I politely sat down and consumed a Big Mac with fries and a soda and an apple pie. On my way out the door I got a "Big Mac for the road" and ate that shit on the school bus. Like a motherfucking boss! A kid in public school who dared to flex eating two Big Macs in one day was a god where I was from. I might as well have been holding a piece of jewelry laced with glistening diamonds. It was a level of wealth reserved for the white kids in the suburbs. It meant Daddy had money.

I was an avid baseball card collector, so I bought more packs of cards. I had all the brands—Donruss, Topps, Fleer—and if I had a little extra money I'd splurge and get Upper Deck. Their cards were glossier and nicer. To me Upper Deck was the Prada of baseball cards. I had magazine subscriptions to *Nintendo Power, Electronic Gaming Monthly, GamePro,* and *MAD* magazine. I wasn't big into popular sneakers, though. In those days, dressing too nice could get you killed, especially in West End. About once or twice a month I'd hear about someone getting killed for their Air Jordans or a Starter jacket. So, to keep from being a target, I would instead wear a pair of Charles Barkleys or Ken Griffey Jrs. They were both respected enough athletes that if you rocked their stuff you didn't get picked on, but not so beloved that someone would take me out over them.

Most of what I spent money on was stuff that my parents weren't really tracking. My father wasn't home half the time, and if he saw me in something new, he just assumed my mother had gotten it for me. Most magazines and videogames I could write off as being something I got for super cheap at a bookfair. The only things my mother noticed occasionally were shirts and shoes, so I still had to allow her the pleasure of telling me no from time to time in a department store when I would beg for something to wear. The middle ground was when I would offer to pay half the cost of the item.

Perhaps my best hustle came from my hatred of math.

My freshman year of high school I failed algebra and had to go to summer school to make up the credit. As much money as I made during the fall raking leaves, the one thing I've always been terrible at is saving money. So by the time summer school came, I was hurting for cash.

I got to summer school ten minutes early every day so I could get a seat by the window. This is where I picked up the habit of people watching. My classroom faced out onto Pearson Ave., a major artery through West End. And there I sat every day for six weeks, six hours a day, looking out the window. I loved watching the TV show that was happening outside as people walked by living their lives.

Across from the school at the time was a Church's Chicken. Every day around 2:00 to 2:30, after lunch rush, a single Church's employee would come out to clean the parking lot. He slowly lumbered around the parking lot looking for things to sweep and pick up, and you could tell it was the worst part of his day. He looked sad like one of those animals in a zoo enclosure.

The downside to that window was on a good day you could smell the chicken. It was torture, because in summer school you got a paper bag lunch consisting of a cold-cut sandwich, some chips, and an apple. I'm pretty sure the meal they gave us was simply leftover food from the county jail the day before. I was in culinary hell. I needed better food. So, one day after classes, I walked across the street and brokered a deal with the Church's Chicken employee.

"I'll clean this parking lot for you every day after summer school, if you give me a free three-piece," I negotiated.

I couldn't even finish my sentence before the guy screamed, "Yes! Shit, little nigga I'll throw in a honey biscuit too." He was thrilled. He got to stay inside in the air-conditioning, and I got myself a proper meal every afternoon. It wasn't too long after this that I negotiated similar deals with two gas stations up the same street. Sweeping and cleaning a parking lot is far easier than raking a yard.

Instead of cash, the gas station clerks would pay me in ten-dollars' worth of candy and write it off as shoplifting. I would then take that candy and sell it at summer school whenever I needed a little cash. The rest I would keep for myself.

I was a freshman in high school on a steady diet of fried chicken and candy bars. No wonder I never went pro in baseball.

This time in my life gave me the confidence that I have to this day to not worry about money. Give me enough time and enough stillness and I will figure it out.

From the day that lady pulled up to the house and asked me to rake her yard, I was gifted one of the most important forms of freedom: financial independence. Those days were the best because I knew that I didn't need my mom and I knew for a fact she didn't have to worry about me. And besides, my mom had enough to worry about in her new home as it was.

■ ■ ■

Tensions between my parents had an ebb and a flow to them. I had never asked my mom why they separated in the first place. It just never felt like something I needed to know. I still feel that way.

For the most part my mother and father always kept to their respective sides of the house and did not intrude upon each other's space. They didn't sleep in the same bedroom and didn't argue a great deal. Part of what kept them from arguing much was their schedules. My dad was gone by the time we got up in the morning, by the time my mom got home from law school at night my dad was headed back out the door to either drink with his buddies or do his evening jazz show, and by the time he got back home we were asleep—assuming he even came home that night.

I grew up with both parents in my home, but it was still kind of like an odd in-house joint-custody type of situation.

On the rare occasions we bonded as a family, it wasn't through the usual conversation of "Hey, how was your week?" or "How are your grades in school?" We bonded over the news. Once or twice a month the stars would align and we'd all be home at the same time and share a meal. My father was a nonstop information vacuum, so the idea of using mealtime to bond was foreign to him. He was never at that table without his newspaper. Between bites of food, my father would point out a story to my mom. They would discuss its complexities and sometimes have a lighthearted debate about the merits of the topic at hand.

This would go on for a few minutes and then the table would fall silent again. Then, a few minutes later, my mother would find an article and point it out to my father and again they would debate. In these moments I saw what had attracted her to him. He was a supremely intelligent man, and conversely, she challenged my father to think deeper and use his logic (and not his anger) to analyze the hypocrisy in some of his opinions. She made him better because she was not impressed by his celebrity and was not so enamored with his charm that she'd allow him to go unchecked.

They were intellectuals who made each other better. But I think that's also what drove my father crazy. The silly lies he told other women simply did not work on my mother, and now that she was in law school she *really* knew how to debate. My father would rather leave the house than lose an argument to my mom. And often the only way to win an argument was to bring money into the conversation.

My father paid most of the bills, and he would pull out that trump card in a heartbeat. He'd scream, "I pay the cost to be the boss! And if you don't like it you know where the motherfucking door is!" Knowing that the bulk of her income was wrapped up in law school tuition and paying back student loans from grad school, the door was never going to be an option.

After these arguments, my mother studied even more furiously, determined to use this time in the house to save money and educate herself toward a better life. I sat in a car with my mother most days as she listened to Bill Handel instructional cassette tapes about the law. Now, you would figure that most middle schoolers would get to listen to some music in the car while riding along with their mother. Nope, not me. It was all Bill Handel, all the time. He was an attorney/radio host who talked about legal issues, but he also recorded these lectures about law—books on tape, essentially. While everyone else in class was talking about N.W.A or the latest LL Cool J song, I was well versed in torts and contract law, and I'd be more than happy to litigate any situations that may arise for you on the playground today.

My father was from an era of Black men who thought if you simply paid all the bills in the house, then that justified any other behavior. He constantly reminded us that he was not to be questioned so long as the lights were on and there was food in the fridge. And if we dared to question him, the punishment wasn't physical, it was fiscal.

Sometimes after a good knock 'em out, drag 'em out argument that lasted a couple of days, my father would deliberately not pay a bill. Gas, or lights. Or he wouldn't be home on a Sunday night to give me lunch money for school the following week. Sometimes he'd be home and flat-out tell me no.

"Get ya lunch money from ya mama since you know so fucking much!" he'd growl.

When you come home to a house with no electricity there's a brief state of confusion, then sadness. But if you come home to a dark house enough times it just becomes business as usual. Between candles and a couple of Eveready flashlights, homework still got done. I always beat my mom home so if it was a day that the lights were out because my dad refused to pay the bill, I would simply call my mom before she got home from work to give her the heads-up so she could grab us some McDonald's.

"Hey, the power is out so the stove isn't working and neither is the microwave."

My mother and I have been through so much together. We adjusted and kept pushing forward.

I don't know what psychological mind games my father thought he was playing by not paying the power bill after a large argument—maybe he wanted us to know that he didn't feel sufficiently appreciated for providing for us—but all it did was drive my mother and me closer together. It also made me want to protect her the way she'd protected me at Olivia's house.

"At least the heat is still on," she'd joke while bumping into some shit in the dark. I'd quickly tag the joke, "Yep, thank God for natural gas."

After a day or two, I'd come home and the lights would be on and the refrigerator would be full of fresh food. My father knew how to win me and my mother back, and that was through our stomachs.

My father never apologized for anything. I don't think I ever heard him say "I'm sorry" to anyone for any reason whatsoever. But he would always fill the house with our favorite foods. The same man who, three days earlier, had told me to get lunch money from my mother would pull up with his Lincoln Continental filled to the brim with bags from Piggly Wiggly.

It'd take me thirty minutes to unload the car, let alone get all of it in the fridge and cabinets. It was a full spread: Entenmann's Sour Cream Pound Cake, oatmeal cream pies, A&W cream soda, 5th Avenue candy bars, and tubs upon tubs of Breyers' then upscale ice cream brand, Marble Classics.

After I was done, I'd pull my mother to the side and joke, "You need to argue with him like this every two weeks so we can keep eating good. Hell, if you get him mad enough, I might get some new sneakers." We'd laugh a little too hard. Sometimes my dad would hear us in the kitchen laughing and wonder what the joke was.

Birmingham galvanized my mother and me. We took different paths, but we were both fearless at this point in our lives and unintimidated by any challenges, including being in a dark house.

Bad things happened, we cracked a joke with each other, and we moved on. It was just the way things were. In many ways, my mother's response to my father's behavior set an example of how I should move through adversity. With my eye on the prize.

In Memphis, I'd never worked a single day in my life. But in Birmingham, I'd been a resident for less than two months and I'd already learned the value of a dollar—and the value of maintaining a sense of humor when you don't have a dollar. Most solutions to the problems I had during those days came from remaining calm, analyzing the world around me, and following my instincts.

I hope the same for you, son.

CHAPTER 4

Thanks a Million

Most homes that I visited in Birmingham seemed to have some degree of dysfunction. None of them seemed ideal. My friends were all children of a parent who was single, or alcoholic, or abusive, or absentee, or overprotective. I can't think of a single time that I ever visited a friend's house or had a sleepover and longed to live in their household instead of my own. I guess dysfunction is all about wearing the shoe that fits you best.

The day I felt this shoe fit most comfortably, the one day when there seemed to be peace and love in our home, was Sunday. The rest of the week might have been tense, but Sundays were calm. It was like how some street gangs have what's called a Sunday truce. No matter what the beef is, no matter what the grievances are, you don't kill on Sundays.

Sunday was the one day we were all together. My mom would cook a proper full breakfast, and no matter where my father was in the city he always seemed to find his way home on Sunday mornings. There wasn't a lot of conversation, but my parents' love of newspapers and our shared quest for information kept us close one day a week.

In the early years of Sunday breakfast, I didn't care that much about reading the newspaper. I would usually bring a *MAD* magazine to the table and read it instead. Then one day, between bites, my father mumbled, "Same shit you're reading in that magazine is in this newspaper."

He flipped the Sunday paper open, revealing its innards. Between all the sales ads and coupons and store flyers was the comics section. I fell in love.

I read all the comics, even the ones I didn't fully understand. I tried desperately to understand *The Far Side,* but I was too young. Same with *Doonesbury* (which I'm still not sure I understand). There was *Garfield* and *Marmaduke* and *Peanuts. Family Circus* wasn't too bad. My absolute favorite was *Calvin and Hobbes.* I used to have stuffed animals and imagine them as real people, so I could totally relate to that fantasy world.

As I grew older, so did my appetite for what was in the paper. Sports was the next progression as I became a more avid baseball and football fan. I wanted to track the Chicago Cubs in the summer and then the Miami Dolphins in the fall.

The lifestyle section didn't appeal to me because it was really just for people with money. It featured television shows I never saw, movies I never watched, restaurants I never dined in, and exotic destinations I'd never travel to, and then jammed in a bunch of ads for products my family could never buy.

The parts of the paper I came to love—and still do—were the advice columns. I was fascinated by other people's problems. They reassured me of the fact that I wasn't the only person dealing with issues. It also was a beautiful window into what people are like and what they desire.

The advice givers were various: a car repair advice columnist; a money and finance guru; Miss Manners, who told southerners how to behave; and the big dog, Dear Abby. The funny thing about Dear Abby was that nothing indicated that she was qualified to be giving advice, but everyone trusted her. People would pour out their hearts to this woman and she would always offer sound and fair advice.

And then there was Percy Ross. Percy was a millionaire philanthropist who had a nationally syndicated column called "Thanks a Million." In the column, he gave away money to random strangers who wrote to him with their various sob stories. In a lot of ways, it was a precursor to GoFundMe, Kickstarter, and other digital forms of soliciting money.

This column intrigued me more than anything else in the paper. I couldn't wrap my head around it. *You telling me he has so much money that he can just give it away?* My idea of a millionaire at that time was Scrooge McDuck from the Disney universe, and he refused to give money to *anyone.* So to see a white person with so much money they could literally give it away was mind-blowing.

The problems people wrote in about to Percy covered a range of ordeals. There were a lot of people with medical debt and people who were just trying to get a computer for their child, or a once-in-a-lifetime trip somewhere. Percy Ross didn't say yes to everyone. Sometimes he would write people back and just say "No." Ask Percy for something too trivial, and instead of giving you the money he would give you a good verbal lashing in the column for all to see. And keep in mind this was back in the day when they would put your full name in the newspaper, so you were on Front Street if you asked for money. It also meant you were on Front Street if Percy rejected you.

No matter how proud you were, or how contrite you were, when you asked, it always felt like you were saying, "Would you please assist me in doing life properly because I am too stupid to know how to do life?"

Percy Ross's column—and the newspaper in general—provided a true window into everything that was happening outside of where

I lived. On Sundays, I got to visit the rest of the world and get a sample of other people's problems.

■ ■ ■

The biggest dustups between my parents weren't about money. They were about respect. One incident is still lodged in my memory.

The only thing my mother ever asked of my father was to be respectful of the home. What she was basically saying was, "I know that you are cheating, but please do not bring those women around here or have my son around them." It was a very odd gentleman's agreement.

Surprisingly, my father generally complied with my mother's request, but every now and then the women did not. And if there was one thing my mother the career educator was capable of, it was teaching somebody a lesson.

The only thing my father loved more than women was his cars. I wouldn't say he collected them, but he was always trading one in to get another. He never had fewer than four. He bought Cadillacs, Lincoln Continentals, Lincoln Town Cars, and a Lincoln Mark VIII. My pops was so tight with the auto dealers in the city, they knew my father's taste and would call him when someone traded in something that he'd like. My dad would scurry out of the house like a firefighter headed to the truck to respond to a call. Sometimes he would pull up to purchase a used Lincoln while the original owner was still in the showroom doing the paperwork for the trade-in.

If he wasn't being tipped off by the car dealerships, then the rest he found from meticulously combing through the classified ads of the newspaper during Sunday breakfast. If he didn't have a speaking engagement at a church, I would often spend Sundays with my father driving all over the city as he looked at used Lincolns for sale from private owners.

He loved those cars. They were truly his peace.

His other peace was Valerie.

Valerie was the woman with whom my father shared two younger children. My father worked hard to make sure I had a relationship with my two younger half brothers. Every other week or so he'd arrange for all of us to do something together. I'd always liked being an only child, but I welcomed the opportunities to hang out with my two younger half brothers because it usually meant we were going to go somewhere fun like Chuck E. Cheese or the Fairgrounds. When I was with my father alone, more often than not his idea of fun was me running errands with him. But when I was with my two younger brothers, we would actually do legit fun things that kids enjoy doing. Through my two younger brothers I was able to experience a different side of my father that I would have never gotten alone. Trips to the pawnshop were replaced with trips to play Putt-Putt golf. I would be well into my thirties before I made the connection that the activities my father sought out when he was with me were different from those he sought out when he was with them. My mother wasn't necessarily crazy about there being two other kids out there, but she had brought me to Birmingham to have more of a father figure, so she never really complained. Everything was cool so long as women didn't come by the house; anything outside of that was a nonissue and not worth the fight.

Some days, my dad would pick me up from baseball practice and take me over to Valerie's house so I could see my younger brothers. Valerie made dinner and we'd sit there and eat like what I guess my father envisioned was some sort of blended family.

Valerie drove my father's two-door blue Mercury Cougar. It was one of his favorites, but he didn't mind her driving it. I think Valerie needed my dad and my dad enjoyed the feeling of being needed. So it worked. My mother never gave him that feeling; she was too busy working on her third degree.

One afternoon, when I was about thirteen years old, Valerie came by our house. She was normally in good spirits, but on this day she was *seething*—so much so that she decided to confront my dad. Whatever it was, it was a conversation that could not wait until the next time he saw her. In her anger, she broke my mother's only rule. She came by the house.

Valerie banged and banged, then kicked, then banged on the front door some more. It was the kind of knocking where you first look out a side window to see whose car is there. My mother looked outside and saw the blue Mercury Cougar, and she knew who was at the door.

My mother opened the front door but not the screen door, making sure to keep distance between herself and Valerie.

"Good afternoon, Joyce. I'm here to see Roy. I don't want any problems with you."

"You have two babies by a married man, you've been had problems with me."

By this time my father had emerged at the door, demanding that my mother mind her business and telling Valerie to get the fuck away from his house. At the same time, my mother was telling Valerie to get the fuck away from her house, while at the same time my father was telling my mother that this wasn't her house, it was his house; while at the same time Valerie reminded my father that this was not his home, her house was his home.

"Both of you can shut the fuck up!" my father said. "I paid the cost to be the boss and, Joyce, you can get the fuck out of my house too."

Whatever reason Valerie had for being at the house could not be articulated clearly through all of the crosstalk. She repeatedly declined my mother's request to leave the premises.

My mother calmly walked away. Valerie and my father then continued to argue through the screen door. About two minutes later, my mother reemerged from a back room with her shoes on and my Little League baseball bat in her hands. It's funny how, when someone's holding a baseball bat, you're suddenly able to speak to them in a calm and respectful manner. Valerie saw the bat and wisely figured it was probably better to table the convo with my father for another time.

"Joyce! I don't want no trouble, Joyce! *I don't want no trouble,*" Valerie pleaded.

My mom wasn't trying to hear none of that shit and stormed out the door. Valerie bolted toward the Mercury Cougar. My father ran out the door in hot pursuit of my mother, but there was no catching her. He was a Black man with a limp. She was a Black woman on a mission. My father never stood a chance.

"You don't come to my home. Can't control what y'all do out there but I'll be damned, bitch, if you're going to come to my home and disrespect me!" my mother screamed.

I'd never seen my mother this upset. Apparently, neither had my father, and neither had the neighbors. Mrs. Murray was now on her front porch watching this unfold. Even the boys selling crack next door to her came outside to see. You know the drama is good when you take a break from selling crack cocaine to see what the commotion is next door. Public arguments are the hood equivalent of live Shakespeare in the Park. The performances are so riveting, you can't turn away.

My mother calmly walked around the car after Valerie like Michael Myers. One lap around the car and Valerie managed to unlock the door. It would take two more trips around the car before she was able to hurriedly jump inside the vehicle, lock the door, and try to start the engine, but it was too late. My mother had found her target, the windshield.

My mother cocked back that baseball bat and unleashed a Ken Griffey Jr.–level swing on the windshield of my father's beloved Mercury Cougar. *Crack!* Shards of glass shot into the air and rained down on the hood like raindrops. My father was such a celebrity, that cars passing by still tooted their horns and waved at him completely unaware that he was in the middle of a domestic dispute.

The windshield was cracked pretty good, but it was still intact. My mother wasn't satisfied, so she cocked back to deliver another shot. Just as she did, Valerie threw the car into gear and tried to speed away. But my father's house sat at the beginning of a dead-end street off a major thoroughfare. So you couldn't speed off because you'd run directly into traffic. Valerie literally traveled about five car lengths from our house to the stop sign. There was traffic coming both ways, and she had nowhere to go. My mother, still at a Michael Myers steady pace, slowly walked up to that gorgeous Mercury Cougar. She calmly patted the barrel of the bat in her hand like a murderer with all the time in the world with his victim. My mother smirked. Valerie screamed. My father cursed. The drug dealers cheered.

"Hit that shit again!" they jubilantly cheered.

My mother went to work.

Windshields, side-view mirrors, door panels, quarter panels, they all met the end of my Easton baseball bat.

As Valerie drove off, the shouts between her and my mother dissipated. The only sound filling the air now was the wailing and cursing from my father. He was furious—not because of the fight but because my mother had taken a baseball bat to his beloved Mercury Cougar.

"Motherfucking bitch, you gon' pay for it! That's my goddamn car, bitch," he screamed.

"We married, you dumb motherfucker! That ain't none of your car, it's *our* car! And in a marriage I can do with *our* car whatever the fuck I choose! There's no such thing as yours or mine in a marriage. It's communal property!" she screamed back.

The Bill Handel law tapes were starting to pay off.

My father stared at her motionless, a calm rage enveloped his face. In his eyes my mother had crossed a line, but we didn't yet know what the penalty for this would be. As the three of us filed back into the house, my father exploded. Inches from my mother's face, he screamed, "I don't know where you get off thinking you can destroy *my* shit I worked hard for, but you are mistaken." She calmly walked past him looking at the barrel of the baseball bat, picking out any pieces of glass, and scraping off some of the paint that had transferred from the car to the bat.

I didn't like the vibes from him being that close, so I inched a little closer to her.

Seeing my movement, my father shot me an incredulous look but backed up out of her face, repeating himself in a cooler tone.

"You are going to pay for what you did to my car."

A couple of days later I came home from school to a house that was unusually cold. I walked around the house and checked all the windows and all the doors. Everything was closed. I then went to check the heaters and realized I did not hear the slow hiss of the gas pilot light. I turned the heat to high. Nothing. The gas had been cut off in the house. I called my mom at work. At this point it was too late in the day to call the gas company. I remember seeing on the news that there were pipe freeze warnings in effect. So it had to have been at least twenty-five degrees Fahrenheit. My father didn't come home that night.

These are the types of temperatures that old people freeze to death in. These are the types of temperatures where the Red Cross hands out space heaters at a community center. It's not until you sleep in a cold home that you realize that your house has too many fucking windows for heat to escape through. My mother and I slept that night in our respective beds with two layers of clothes and two blankets. I woke up that morning and I could literally see my breath.

That second day, I went to school and came back home, still no heat. This for sure answered the question of whether I'd rather be in a home with no lights or no heat. Give me heat every time. My mom came home that night with two space heaters from work. We angled them both at the dining room table to create one little heat zone at the kitchen table for us to do work, kind of in the same way

NFL teams in the winter create warming zones on the bench for their players.

We had electricity, so the stove still worked. We had a perfectly great dinner, while at the same time sniffling because it was so cold. I would do my homework and then head upstairs to play Nintendo in freezing temperatures. But you can't. It's impossible to focus. The space heaters were allowed to stay on until we went to bed, and then we had to turn them off for fear of burning to death in a house fire.

Another night alone in the dark and the cold.

My mother told me the gas company said they had received a request to disconnect the service. To reconnect service and pay the remaining balance would cost about $500. We needed $500, and we needed it fast.

I went to my stash of all the money I had saved up from all my hustles, but I was low—$100. We were far into winter, so there were no more leaves to be raked. My mother refused to take it. That night I fell asleep again to the sounds of my mother soliciting her friends for money. The next morning, I racked my brain over where I could find $400 in one day. I decided that there was only one person I could turn to: Percy Ross.

When I got home that night, I started writing a letter to Percy, explaining to him that I was a Black kid freezing in my father's home. I explained how I'd started my leaf-raking company, and how hard my mother worked, and how she just needed a break. Though my father talked a lot in his speeches about the Black man not needing the white man, and I believed a lot of that, I was also tired of freezing in my own room. Never before had I written a clearer letter. I dropped that bad boy in the mail and waited patiently for a check from Percy.

Chest filled with confidence, I went downstairs to my mother the next morning.

"I got you, Mom. Just give me a week and I got you."

That afternoon we came home to a warm house and a fridge full of groceries. My father was sitting in the living room. He waited for me to thank him. I didn't say a word, just went upstairs. When my mom came home, she came to my room.

"What did you mean yesterday when you said, 'Just give me a week'? Since we don't need the money now, how were you planning to get the money?"

Too embarrassed to tell her what I had done, I made up some story about a painting job I had found. She seemed to be satisfied enough with my answer, so she went on her way. Still, I was excited. Surely "Black kid freezing" was enough for him to send $400. This way I would have $400 in the house at any given time to back up my mother if—or when—my dad pulled his bullshit again.

Every week after I mailed my letter, I scanned the Percy Ross column like a hawk. I didn't know the logistics of how the newspaper column worked. Did they run the letter first and then send the check? Would someone call to verify the story? I figured I'd find out when I heard from him. After about three months reading letter after letter written to Mr. Ross asking for stuff that I thought was not more important than a Black kid freezing in his home, I thought to myself, *Fuck Percy Ross.*

Before I'd written that letter, I'd always tried to figure out how to do things on my own—and I had. But this time, I couldn't solve the problem myself, so I'd finally accepted that we need other people. I'd listened to the people who'd always told me, "If you need help, just ask." I'd reached out to the only person I thought could help me, Percy Ross. And he'd failed me.

I hadn't asked Percy for money for Space Camp or some stupid shit. I was freezing. Like, freezing. I'd asked for help, and the motherfucker didn't even give me the dignity of a reply. As an adult I can see now that he was a nationally syndicated columnist who probably got swamped with requests for money. The chances that he even saw that letter were slim to none. But at the time, the message I received was simple: No one cares about your problems. In that moment, I knew the only person who was going to help me was me. That letter to Percy Ross was the last time I asked anyone other than my parents for money.

I'm not sure how much better or worse off this decision made me, but my run-in with Percy Ross sealed my fate as an independent person. No one was going to swoop in to save me—not Percy Ross, not my father, not my mother. I was free to fly or fall on my own terms. If it was going to get done, I would have to do it alone.

Be very careful wielding this sword, son. It's a gift and a curse, a secret weapon and a tumor. It is the best of me, it is the worst of me, and I've lived with it ever since those freezing cold nights at home.

Don't be afraid to ask for help. It's okay to need people. I fear that I learned too much self-reliance in Birmingham, and will probably always struggle to accept help. But I share this now so hopefully you don't have to.

CHAPTER 5

The Cook and the Creep

When I was a teenager, the only thing I hated more than needing money was needing a ride. When I needed money, I could figure out a way to earn it (or, in later days, steal it). I can't think of a time that I've ever borrowed money from anyone, ever. But when I needed a ride, there was no way to hustle my way out of it. Mass transit in Birmingham was never going to be better than a car. I enjoyed riding the school bus when I was younger—good times and great laughs—but like most high school kids, I longed for my own car.

I would have rather asked someone for *anything* else than a ride. When you ask people for a ride, you can *feel* them thinking about it, almost looking you up and down and deciding whether or not to be a blessing. They're literally doing the calculations in front of you.

There's one thing about Black people—they will give you a ride somewhere, but they will let it be known they really don't want to give you a ride. The conversation went the same every time.

"Hey, man, can you give me a ride home?"

"Where do you live?"

"I live in West End."

"What part of West End?"

"Off South Park Road and Pearson Avenue."

Now, once you told somebody the exact location of where you lived, you could see them doing the geography in their head, calculating distances and trajectories like a NASA scientist as they figured out how much of an inconvenience you were about to be.

Also, at this point in the conversation, there was usually an awkward pause, which was an opportunity for you, the broke bastard with no car, to politely say, "I will give you five dollars' gas money."

The polite thing to do was to offer up gas money and hope deep down they didn't accept it.

I constantly had to bum rides between work and baseball practice. In high school, we didn't practice on campus because there was no room for a field. Instead, we usually commuted fifteen to twenty minutes to various city parks around Birmingham, most of them even farther from my home than my high school was.

Coach would make the varsity guys with a car responsible for getting the car-less junior varsity guys to practice every day. Now, the whole point of having a cool car in high school was to cruise around and impress women. Kind of hard to do that when you have a car full of freshmen. As a result, most of the varsity players gave us a ride, but it was clear they didn't love it.

When I was a sophomore, the senior everyone wanted to ride with was Johnny Edwards. Johnny was smooth. He had a maroon 1994 Nissan Altima with a booming sound system. When you left school you'd race to the senior parking lot to get a ride with him. You didn't need to look for Johnny Edwards—you could feel the bass reverberating from his car for a two-mile radius.

The only person with a better sound system than Johnny was our teammate Levaughn. He could barely touch the knob on his radio and it felt like sitting inside of a rocket reverberating before liftoff. Levaughn had this electric-blue station wagon with deep-tinted windows and these low-profile tires that brought the car so close to the ground that an ant couldn't crawl underneath. They'd have to go around. If you could get a ride to baseball practice with either of them you were in for a good-ass time. The tiebreaker most days was that Levaughn tended to play a lot of West Coast rap. I loved Ice Cube and Eazy-E and Too Short, but 1994 was the rise of Outkast and Johnny bumped their debut album, *Southernplayalisti-cadillacmuzik* . . . Every. Fucking. Day.

These two guys were who you wanted to be riding with to practice. It boiled down to which genre of music you were in the mood for that day:

'Cause just like Waco, I can take fo'
ATF, to they death

—ICE CUBE, "REALLY DOE," 1993

All the players came from far and wide
Wearin' afros and braids, kickin' them gangsta rides

—OUTKAST, "PLAYER'S BALL," 1994

Chill in the park or kill federal agents? Two distinctly different sounds.

The music Levaughn played and the volume he played at always made you feel like you were on your way to do a drive-by shooting and not baseball practice.

Johnny, on the other hand, had the windows down and a cool breeze flowing through the car, and you'd feel like you could flirt with any girl in the city. We'd kick back with our elbows out the window singing along to "Player's Ball."

It was a beautiful time.

The end of baseball practice was a much different story. As soon as we were free to go home, seniors sprinted for their cars as we underclassmen scanned the parking lot to see if our parents had arrived yet.

My mother and father generally rotated week to week on picking me up. One night, after a downtown practice, there was some miscommunication between them and neither one came to get me. There were no cellphones back then, so you kind of had to stand there in the cold and hope. By the time I realized that my parents weren't coming to get me, it was after the last city bus headed to my side of town had already departed from the downtown hub.

High school baseball season starts at the end of January, so it was a solid thirty degrees that night as I stood outside, shivering in baseball pants, waiting for the headlights of either of my parents' cars to break the seal on the darkness that enveloped me on the baseball field. My coach would normally sit and wait, but I assured him my parents were coming and urged him to head home. Six thirty turned into seven o'clock. Seven o'clock turned into seven thirty.

There had been an incident the previous season where I took a ride home from a teammate because I thought that my father was not coming. Turns out he was coming, but he was late and had no way of telling me he was late. When he got home that night, he cursed me out for wasting his time.

I was hesitant to leave the baseball field that night because I wasn't sure if this was another one of those scenarios. The frosty hypothermic air begin to make its way through my thin baseball pants, so I decided to layer my school clothes on top of my baseball uniform, but there's only so much that blue jeans and baseball pants double-layered can do against a twenty-five-degree wind chill. I called the house from a pay phone and no one answered. So I did the only thing I knew that I could do. I started walking.

What would've been a twenty-minute drive I figured would be about a ninety-minute walk in thirty-degree temps.

About halfway through the walk my hands were essentially frozen in place, and I was openly shivering. Anger had sustained me for the first half of the walk. Just as my frustration was running low, on Sixth Avenue South, across from a Birmingham police station, I came to a liquor store.

It was the only thing open on that street, and I knew that street well. It was going to be another forty-five minutes before I got to another retail district where I could warm up. So I decided to stand inside the liquor store for as long as I could—at least until I could get the feeling back in my fingers and my toes. The store owner didn't make much of me to begin, figuring I was just in there to buy a soda.

After about twenty minutes, it was clear to the store owner that I wasn't going to buy anything, so he shooed me out of the store. As I was coming out, a larger heavyset Black man walked in. He saw me walk out into the darkness of the night still shivering. I could feel him stare at me. I looked back at him briefly, and I could see him making the NASA calculations in his mind. He could go on about his business, or he could ask me where I was headed and offer me a ride. He stared at me for a second, then turned and went into the store. So much for that. Off into the darkness I continued.

About two blocks later, a car slowly pulled up alongside me. It was the man from the liquor store. I could see the apprehension in his face, but I could see he had made a decision that he was going to engage me in conversation and get to the bottom of my situation. He behaved with the reluctance of a person who knows his dead grandmother is watching him.

Between sips of the bourbon he'd just purchased, he started the convo. "Hey! Hey, little nigga! Where the fuck are you going in all this cold?"

I said, "I'm going to West End."

He said, "Nigga, West End? On foot that's at least another forty-five minutes."

I said, "I know."

He continued to creep alongside me as I continued to walk. He took another sip of his bourbon, then paused. Then all of a sudden, he rummaged around in the car and found the cap to the bottle of bourbon and reluctantly screwed it back on.

"Fuck it, man. C'mon, lil nigga, get in the car. I'll take you where you need to go."

I said, "No, thank you, I'm good."

"Nigga, ain't nobody trying to touch yo bootyhole! I'm a drunk, not a rapist." As funny as it was that he felt the need to say that, it was actually calming and reassuring to hear. I don't know any child kidnapper that would break the ice by proclaiming that they were a drunk. I thought about my safety for all of two seconds and hopped in the car, and he gave me a ride home.

The ride was silent. The man was almost annoyed that he was forced to stop his drunken evening to be a guardian angel for some teenager who was about to go strolling through gang territory. The part of town I was crossing into was a little rough. Even if you aren't in a gang, being in a neighborhood where no one recognizes you could leave you open to a minimum of having your lunch money taken or something.

My drunken guardian angel got me home in less than ten minutes. When I walked in the house, my parents were both sitting on the couch, cozy, fucking watching *Wheel of Fortune*. I was freezing and furious. "Thanks for picking me up." Rather than apologize, the first thing my father did was say, "You better watch who the fuck you're talking to." Then my parents both looked at each other and simply said, "I thought you were picking him up."

My mother didn't apologize either. Instead she met me with a question.

"Who just gave you a ride home?" she asked. To which I replied, "The dude I met at the liquor store."

"The *liquor store*?" my dad screamed. I snapped right back, "*Yes!* I was at the liquor store getting warm because both of y'all forgot that you had a child tonight." My mom ran back to the front porch just in time to get a quick glimpse of the stranger who'd brought me home. He was still in the driveway enjoying a celebratory sip of his bourbon.

My mother's jaw dropped. I walked around her and gave him a thumbs-up to let him know I was in the house safely. He returned the gesture, took another long swig of his bourbon, threw his car in reverse, and headed off into the night.

As he pulled away, my mother mumbled, "You got a ride home from a goddamn drunk."

"Yep," I said, "but better to meet a drunk than a kidnapper."

"Don't be funny, boy, it's child molesters out there."

"So long as he was gonna do it somewhere warm, I might've let him do it," I snapped back.

My mother wanted to be mad, but she had to respect the exchange. My father finally let out a chuckle.

But that's how it was asking people for a ride. There was always an odd tension in the transaction and I hated it. I remember in high school, I had this job at Baskin-Robbins ice cream shop inside of Western Hills Mall in the Birmingham suburb of Fairfield. I was fifteen years old, and the store was run by a manager in his early twenties named Anthony. Anthony was a great guy, and very suave as well. He had a deep voice, a nice goatee, and perfectly manicured nails. The female employees from every store in the mall came in when he was working and made sure to get a scoop of ice cream. I would step in and attempt to serve the ladies, and they would politely wait for Anthony to serve them. He had a cool car, he smelled good. Anthony was the fucking man.

On top of all this, Anthony was a hard worker and an excellent manager. He stayed on top of us about side work and always had the store in tip-top shape. Working closing shifts with him was hilarious, though. Most stores will close at 9:00, and then there's another thirty to forty-five minutes of shutdown work to do. Anthony had it down to a science that side work was usually done before we closed. We could literally lock the doors at 9:00 and be walking out at 9:02, the reason being, if Anthony was able to close the store early, then he could flirt with the women who were ending their respective shifts as well.

So needless to say, me needing the occasional ride home was throwing a wrench in his plans. Anthony had two choices. He could keep me with him, like a tag-along little brother, and flirt as best he could but know deep down he wasn't going to be able to break off with any of the women to grab drinks or have a parking lot make-out session because he still had to take me home. His second option was to rush me home, fifteen minutes away, and rush back to the mall and hope that the women hadn't yet left the mall.

He hated doing it, but he always did it. Reluctant benevolence is the most sincere kind. It's insistent benevolence that you have to be cautious of.

I learned this lesson again two years later working in a hospital kitchen. Mr. Ed was the first openly gay man I ever knew. I had classmates as early as middle school who were for sure gay, but they never came out and said it, though they didn't pretend to be straight either.

Openly gay men weren't a foreign concept to me, albeit their acceptance in the super conservative southern culture was still slow to happen. I'd had my first encounters with openly gay people the year before at sixteen years old. I worked a late shift at the Subway sandwich shop, which was in the Five Points South Arts District of Birmingham. It was a nice little three- to four-block stretch of bars, tattoo shops, drug addicts, goth kids, black fingernail polish, white people who thought they were witches, the homeless, and some

Black people who were starting to ride skateboards. Five Points South was the place for countercultures and rebels. It was filled with artistic types and all the kids who hated school enough to not go, but not enough to walk in with a shotgun and shoot it up. Among the mélange of characters that stumbled into my shop for a sandwich were sometimes male sex workers. Some were dressed in drag, some not. They were on a first-name basis with all of us, and in between bites of their food would tell harrowing tales from turning tricks that night: encounters of barely escaping a robbery, or a customer trying to sneak and take the condom off, or some skinhead that was trying to lure them into an alley to beat with a pipe. I'm not sure how my other sixteen-year-old classmates spent their Friday nights, but I spent mine feeding a collection of societal rejects for $4.50 an hour. As traumatic as I'm sure it all was, they approached it with so much humor it was hard to see the trauma behind their jokes.

But by and large, those years at Subway showed me the humanity in every type of person. It took the mask off of a lot of people that I was told were terrible. There was a lot of open homophobia at that time, and I observed that some gay men could clock the homophobia and use it to manipulate the behaviors of the people around them for their own amusement. They might deliberately brush an arm up against a drunk Christian as they exited the restaurant. And you would see that person scrambling to get to the restroom to wash their arm as if it were going to fall off, only to be told by me and my coworkers that the restroom was closed because a heroin addict had taken a shit on the floor and we hadn't had a chance to clean it up yet because we were dealing with the 2:00 A.M. bar rush. Many nights that was the truth.

My time at Subway had prepared me to interact and communicate with just about any type of person. When I started working in the cafeteria of a rehab hospital a year later, there was nothing that Mr. Ed could say or do that would surprise me. The one thing I most clearly remember about him was how loud he was. This was a man who lived his entire life at ninety decibels. Flamboyantly gay in mid-'90s homophobic, Jesus-loving Alabama, he lived life with no apologies and was thrilled to be alive. He was funny and charismatic. He was loud and rambunctious. He could belt out Luther Vandross or Mahalia Jackson while assembling some of the best-prepared meals in all of Alabama. And ten minutes later he'd be talking about sexual conquests that he had made the night before. He would never name names, but he also talked about how many people in Birmingham that we thought were straight were actually gay. The term *down low* had yet to enter our vocabulary as a society, but Mr. Ed was already showing us that some straight men weren't so straight.

He would spend half his shift working the grill and the other half trying to sell people on the orgasmic wonders of being gay. "I'm telling y'all, don't knock it 'til you try it! It's fucking amazing. You get you a good nigga who know how to throw that dick the right way. Baby, I'm telling you, you'll never go back."

"You need to try some pussy, man," a straight male coworker retorted.

Without missing a beat, Mr. Ed snapped back, "What makes you think I never tried it? I *did* try it. Baby, the last piece of pussy I had was the day I was born, and I kicked that bitch on the way out."

The kitchen was fucking howling with laughter. We were all doubled over.

Hearing a thirty-something-year-old gay man argue with someone else in the kitchen about vaginal versus anal sex wasn't exactly the type of convo my sixteen-year-old mind was ready to hear. But you work in food service, you're gonna grow up fast. The conversations made some of our more conservative coworkers uncomfortable, but this was long before the days of reporting someone to HR because you didn't like the jokes.

My car continued to be unreliable, so usually two, three days a month I needed to bum a ride from someone at the hospital who lived on the west side. I had a coworker who lived close to me, and more often than not we were on the same shift. So if my car was in the shop, I would catch a ride with her.

One night, my supervisor, Mr. Donovan, found out that I was riding with her and insisted that I ride with him instead. The offer didn't make sense to me because Mr. Donovan didn't live as far into the west side as this coworker did, but he insisted. And it seemed safe to me. Mr. Donovan was a suave man in his early thirties who wore a full suit to work in the kitchen. If you saw him, you would assume he was a lawyer, not a man making sure there was enough Ensure and applesauce in dry stock.

The rides home with Mr. Donovan were the opposite of any ride I'd ever gotten from any other Black man. He was pleasant, he asked me constant questions about my life, and he encouraged me to ask him questions. He was polite and he was kind. Sometimes we'd pull off in a gas station. He'd buy me whatever soda or drink or candy I wanted. It got to a point where he already knew what my favorite snacks and candies were, and he would bring them to me at work and leave them in the break room.

Mr. Donovan gave me a ton of advice about life, women, saying no to drugs. I definitely felt like I was getting something out of the relationship, and I eventually found myself looking forward to our rides home together. It was nice to have someone so caring. It was such a great departure from the usual tension on these types of car rides. Also there was something about him that was far more friendly than it was authoritative. Growing up in a city as Black as Birmingham, your interactions with most Black men are very authoritative. Your teacher, your coach, your pastor, your scoutmaster, your supervisor—at every turn it's just a Black man who can't wait to tell you what to do. Mr. Donovan felt more like a big brother.

One day a few months later, when my car was down again, Mr. Donovan offered to give me a ride home, same as always. On the way to my house, he said, "Hey, man, I hope you don't mind, but I need to stop at my house real quick on the way." I said, "Sure, no problem."

He pulled up to his home on the outskirts of the west side of Birmingham. He was actually pretty close to the same liquor store I'd warmed up in that night my parents forgot to pick me up. Between a handheld videogame system and a few magazines in my backpack, I had more than enough media to entertain me while Mr. Donovan ran into the house to do whatever he needed to do. I had no intention of coming inside.

He said, "Oh, no, man, you can come in." I said, "No, it's fine. I'll stay out here. Just do what you got to do, and I'll read some stuff here in the car."

To which he countered, "Oh no, man, I'm going to be at least fifteen to twenty minutes. You should come in. This neighborhood isn't safe, and I don't want you getting kidnapped or something crazy."

I conceded the safety point and went into the house. It was a pretty simple home for a thirty-year-old man. Basic couch, a rug, a TV.

"Have a seat on the couch," he said. "I'll be out in about ten or fifteen minutes."

"Cool," I said.

I heard him walk to the back of the house and I heard a conversation. It was for sure two men. Mr. Donovan came back through the living room to grab something from the kitchen. At this point, he no longer had his shirt on. He still had on his work pants from our shift. He looked at me and said, "I'll be right back. Oh, by the way, Mr. Ed is here."

Mr. Donovan headed to the back, and out came Mr. Ed wearing nothing but a bath towel. His skin was still wet, freshly showered. You could feel the humidity leaving his body. Mr. Ed said hello, but he could see me processing the fact that he and Mr. Donovan lived together. I was trying to do the math in my head on whether they were a couple or just roommates. It was hard to figure out at the time. I hadn't had enough interactions with gay people socially to even know this was a thing that could happen. But in the assumptions of the streets, two grown men over thirty living together meant you were gay, even if you weren't. I had seen gay people before, but I had never seen an actual gay couple. So I couldn't quite put together what I was looking at.

Mr. Ed sat down on the couch, next to where I was sitting, for about five or ten minutes. He tried to make small talk as I flipped through a magazine and tried to not look at this man who was basically naked. About ten minutes later, Mr. Donovan came out, and *he was wearing nothing but a fucking bath towel now too!*

He plopped down on the other side of me and tried to place his hand on my leg.

"So, do you have a girlfriend, Roy?" he asked.

"Yeah," I said.

Mr. Ed asked, "Have you had sex with her yet? Still a virgin?"

Mr. Donovan then asked, "How much do you know about sex?"

Mr. Ed added, "Is there anything you've ever wanted to learn about sex? About your body?"

It took me longer than it should have to realize how uncomfortable shit had just gotten.

I looked at Mr. Ed, then looked at Mr. Donovan and said, "Hey, my mom is expecting me. I need you to take me home. You can't take me home, let me know. I'll walk up to that liquor store and get a ride. The owner knows me."

Mr. Ed looked at Mr. Donovan. They stared at one another for a second as if deciding what to do next. Whatever plans they had for me they decided to abort. Mr. Donovan took a long breath, then in a resigned tone said, "I'll get dressed."

I went outside and waited for him. He came outside dressed to the nines, clearly for some event that he was headed to. He gave me a ride home in silence. No more small talk, no more chitchat, no stopping for snacks.

Work was awkward after that too. He never volunteered to take me home from work again. Even now as an adult, I remain leery of anyone who is too eager to do something for me, especially when it's not clear what they want in return. It's not to say that there aren't truly happy benevolent people in this world. I simply have to process them through a second layer of character assessment.

Everything is about patterns. If you don't pay attention to what's going on around you, you can look up and suddenly be in a shit situation before you realize it. It's important to keep your head on a swivel. Doubt everything you see. And when something looks good, trust but verify. Be wary of people who are too nice or do not make their needs/wants known, be it professionally or romantically. Watch them more closely.

Mr. Donovan was too nice. He and Mr. Ed clearly had run this play on many a teenager before me. It was too smooth, too scripted. It's entirely possible they were trying to tell me it was okay to be gay or curious or something. Maybe they saw it as a nice gesture, but at its core it was still two grown men sitting down with nothing on but a towel next to a fucking teenager. At minimum the shit was *odd* if not criminal. The fact that neither offered me a ride home again after that left me feeling it wasn't an innocent occurrence.

I've never had a problem declining doing anything that I didn't want to do. And I've never had a problem leaving somewhere that I did not want to be. No matter how awkward it feels, do the right thing. Remove yourself from any situation that doesn't serve you.

After the awkward bath towel encounter, Mr. Donovan dropped me off at the house and I walked in the same as always.

"Who gave you a ride home this time? Was it that drunk again?" my mom sarcastically asked.

"No ma'am, this time it was one of them child rapists you be telling me about," I said.

"Well, at least he wasn't driving drunk, so I guess that's a step up," she sniped back at me.

Until she reads this page in this book, my mother will never know I was actually telling the truth. We both shared a smirk at each other's dark joke and I trotted upstairs to play my videogame. Sarcasm was the way we processed most things, no matter how wild they were. Crack a joke, learn the lesson, and move on.

CHAPTER 6

The Legend of Cocaine Mike

Addiction has never run in my family. We're more of a high cholesterol, high blood pressure, high blood sugar type of family when it comes to genetics. So maybe the addiction is junk food. But it's never been narcotics. Thankfully, drugs didn't appeal that much to me as a teenager. I didn't even need a D.A.R.E. officer to tell me this. Public schools in the '90s were dominated by the "Drug Abuse Resistance Education" curriculum, with some police officer going from classroom to classroom to tell children how bad drugs were and how "nothing good ever happens on drugs."

But I never needed that lesson when it came to not trying drugs. For me, the reasoning for not trying most drugs was simple. I always wanted to be on the go; I always wanted to be moving and shaking, and everyone I knew who smoked joints was the opposite of this.

I tried to drink only once in high school, and that's because I thought it would make me better at baseball. I had a couple of teammates who would sneak a few sips of Wild Irish Rose or Mad Dog

20/20 before stepping in the batter's box, and then they'd hit that ball farther than they did when they were sober. I immediately started viewing alcohol as a performance-enhancing drug. It wasn't even about getting a buzz. I wanted to be better at baseball.

On the way to practice one day, I made a quick detour to the gas station that would sell to minors and had a few sips of Mad Dog 20/20 in the parking lot. Not only was I too drunk to see the ball, but I was also too drunk to catch the ball, which is an important part of playing first base. After three or four balls nearly hit my face because I could not hold my glove up properly, I feigned a pulled muscle and rode out my buzz on the bench.

I wasn't around cannabis growing up, but when I got to college, not only did everyone smoke weed, everyone sold weed. For all the hustling I did in college, selling drugs never crossed my mind. It never seemed worth the trouble. I had a roommate when I was living in the dorms who sold weed, but I ended up making as much money as he did every week, and I was working as a server at a Shoney's restaurant.

I had too much of a work ethic to get into cannabis once I got fully into stand-up comedy after college. I'm not saying it's not possible to be productive smoking weed, but the comedians I was around who were always high never seemed to be doing anything, career-wise. They were funny, but most lacked what I define as ambition. For this reason, I've always seen cannabis as a creative liability for me. I've never ingested it in any form. I've had magic mushrooms a few times. And I tried ayahuasca on a two-day retreat but bailed after the first day because it was emotionally overwhelming. But that's about it.

I've also never done cocaine. But there was one day when I did consider it.

The hospital cafeteria I was working at with Mr. Ed and Mr. Donovan was a small rehab hospital in Birmingham. The facility was for people recovering from a lot of orthopedic-type surgeries: ACLs, backs, rotator cuffs, et cetera. It was also, from time to time, for major high-profile athletes who were in town to take advantage of Birmingham's superior sports medicine programs. It wasn't uncommon to see an elderly woman hobbling down the hall to rehab and right next to her a World Series MVP pitcher.

Because the hospital was popular with athletes, it had a weight room, a swimming pool, and even a full-sized basketball court. The U.S. men's Paralympic wheelchair basketball team trained there, but when the team wasn't training, the basketball court was pretty much a ghost town.

Depending on the day, and whether the person running the gym was a snitch, you could go down to the gym before or after your shift and play a game of pickup basketball with whoever was down there. If you were on the clock, however, you weren't supposed to go to the gym, even on your lunch break. This was a hard rule to follow because working in the cafeteria afforded you a lot of downtime.

I worked as a food porter in the dietary department, which prepared all the meals for every patient in the building, be it some eighty-year-old retiree who had just gotten a hip replacement or an NFL Hall of Famer in town for ACL surgery. Porters distributed said meals and then, an hour later, retrieved food trays, cleaned them, and reset the clean dishes around the kitchen for use again.

Generally there would be three porters working: two men to distribute and retrieve food trays and a third man to break down the dirty dishes that had been returned from each floor. Breaking down the dishes was essentially the process of sorting everything that was dirty on a patient's tray into the appropriate pile—plates, cups, silverware, et cetera—then racking like items together to be run through the industrial dishwasher. The job could be done by two men if they both worked quickly and efficiently, but it was definitely not the preferred way to go about things.

At the rehab hospital I had a coworker who, for the sake of this story, I'll call Mike. Mike was in his early thirties, but the stresses of life and two divorces made him look no younger than fifty years old in the face. He was a Black man, shorter than me, and I stood only five foot nine at that point. His furrowed brow always suggested an intensity of feelings and thoughts happening behind his super-bright white eyes, which were always bugged out as if an optometrist were holding a flashlight an inch from his retinas, or as if he'd just heard something he couldn't believe. A lifetime of coffee and cigarettes had taken a toll on his teeth, and you could smell it too. The only thing more brown than his teeth were his gnarled fingernails. His work uniform was always dirty. I don't think he ever washed it, and if he did, he for sure did not wash his body. Must sliced its way through that fabric and followed him around like an evil spirit.

We weren't bosom buddies, but we were not at odds, plus the job moved so fast there wasn't that much time for sustained conversation outside of cracking a quick joke or two. The process for meal construction was the same for all three meals of the day. Food plates would be fitted nicely into plate warmers and set on a tray that slowly inched down a rickety conveyor belt, like the chassis of a naked automobile inching its way through an assembly line. Next to the plate was the multiple-choice menu filled out by a patient the day before. The plate would slowly make its way past person after person who added entrees, side items, and desserts to it based on the dietary selections on the menu. By the time this plate reached the end of the assembly line, a carefully curated meal had been assembled. An insulating top was thrown on the plate and the tray was placed in one of four huge tray carts, each cart designated for a different wing of the hospital.

Once the cart was loaded down with about thirty to forty food trays, the porters' work began. These carts were about the same size as a refrigerator lying on its side but weighed twice as much because of all the food, heating trays, and beverages inside. Mike and

I had to push these big-ass aircraft carriers down the hallway to nurses on each respective wing. To get the behemoth rolling, you would squat low and push with your legs like a defensive lineman shoving in the trenches trying to get to the quarterback. Step by step, these big eighteen-wheelers would slowly get into motion. The nurses would handle distributing the food trays to the respective patients because they also had to add whatever pills the patient was supposed to be taking with their meal to the tray. The porters would return sixty minutes later to begin the painstaking process of retrieving the trays from each room.

Tray retrieval was where Mike shone. Mike knew that the quicker we retrieved the trays, the quicker we got to the dish room. And the quicker we got to the dish room, the more time he had to disappear into the gym and play basketball before it was time to set up for the next meal of the day. If we had three porters on duty, Mike would sneak off to the gym while two porters worked the dish room. Most of the basketball games in the gym were for money.

Mike didn't care who was down on the basketball court. He wanted to play and he wanted to play for money. He would play doctors, physical therapists, janitors. He would even play the visiting family members of hospital patients. Imagine sitting there day after day grieving your healing loved one and a sweaty-ass dishwasher walks in and challenges you to a game of twenty-one. Anything to get your mind off your sadness, I guess.

As the weeks and months dragged on, Mike became more and more obsessed with being in the gym or flirting with the nurses. For the most part, I never complained. But this one day, it was just me and Mike. There was no third porter. Mike was flagrantly disregarding his duties, and I started feeling like he was taking advantage of my youth. When I was there, Mike's work ethic was different; he just didn't give a fuck. I started to hate going to that job every weekend because I knew I was going to be doing most of the work, and it became exhausting. And I couldn't even complain to my supervisor, Mr. Donovan, because he and the cook were salty that I hadn't been down with their naked couch adventures. I had gotten cold shoulders from them since then. I couldn't tell Mike where to go or what to do, so I set out on the hospital floor to collect dirty trays from 150 hospital beds.

Sweat ran down my face as I raced from room to room, snatching trays off the tables. Some patients were still in the middle of eating their meal and I stood awkwardly close to them, rushing them to finish. The real horror came when I got back to the dish room with four carts, each holding thirty to forty meal trays. Collecting the trays could be a one-man job, but not breaking down the carts and washing them in the dish room. I fell behind and Mr. Donovan became more and more impatient. "What's going on? What's going on? We need them plates. We need them plates. What's going on?" I knew it was urgent because Mr. Donovan hadn't talked to me this much since he was walking around in a bath towel.

The water in an industrial dishwasher could be anywhere from 130 to 150 degrees. The steam that came out at the end had to be closer to 150. Beads of sweat traversed my eyebrows and dripped into my eyes. I had to work through the sting. I was way behind.

It got so bad that my supervisor actually put on an apron and started helping me. He asked, "Man, where's Mike?" I had covered for Mike too many times. Today was the last straw. I said, "Man, he's either out back trying to fuck one of them nurses or he's downstairs playing ball." My supervisor snatched his apron off and marched out of the dish room. About ten minutes later, he returned with Mike. Mike's uniform was soaked in sweat. Either he'd run a marathon or he had been playing basketball. He just stared at me, snatched an apron off the wall, and got to work.

As soon as our supervisor walked off, Mike hauled off and slapped me. *Thwap!* It stung a little extra because his hands were wet and my face was still soaked in sweat. "Motherfucker, don't you *ever* worry about what another man is doing. Worry about what the fuck you can do and do that, because what you can do is all you can do. It don't fucking matter what another man is doing."

As quickly as he said what he said, Mike took a step back from me, and out of his pocket he pulled a little vial of cocaine. He tapped a little bit of it onto his knuckle and snorted it into oblivion. He took a couple of insurance inhales into the same nostril to make sure none of the product fell back out of his nose. He then turned to me and simply said, "Get out the way and watch the master."

Mike refused my help and insisted on doing the last two carts of trays by himself. This meant he had to take every tray off the cart individually, clean the food off it, rack the dirty dishes for washing, run each rack through the dishwasher, take the clean dishes out of the dishwasher, stack those dishes, and then redistribute them to their appropriate spots throughout the kitchen.

I did as I was told and just observed. And God is my witness, this short, sweaty tobacco-breath goblin, high on cocaine, accomplished in twenty minutes what it should take two men to do in forty-five. I've never seen anybody work so fast and focused and efficient as Mike did that day. He was no longer just Mike, he was Cocaine Mike. He was a fucking warrior. An alter ego. A man who came down from the Planet Cocaine to show the world his super-powers. He wasn't even waiting for the dishes to cool off before he racked them out of the dishwasher. I guess those calloused hands could not feel the searing 150 degree heat that was radiating off those plates. The whole time I was watching Mike work, I stood there and all I could think to myself was, *That D.A.R.E. officer was a fucking* liar! *There* are *good things that can happen on drugs.* That officer had never met Cocaine Mike. I started jokingly wondering to myself, *Maybe I* should *look into cocaine. Is this why I am so slow at work?*

But there's a real lesson, a *better* lesson, here. I snitched on Mike because I thought it would get him reprimanded and maybe even fired. I was jealous because I was doing more work than someone else instead of just focusing on what I was hired to do. But nothing happened. It was as if it had never happened. What I didn't understand at the time was that when you're good at what you do, like truly stellar, no one cares why you are good. They only care that you're good. There is a different set of rules.

When he was done, Mike took off his apron, picked up his basketball, and looked back at me, and said, "Class is dismissed. Now take the trash out to the dumpster, you little motherfucker."

That was when I decided to be the best at my job no matter where I worked, so that I too could operate above the law—but without cocaine. And it was the last time I ever snitched on anyone. Because all I can do is what I can do, and since that day I only focus on that. Thanks, Cocaine Mike.

CHAPTER 7

The Final Baked Potato

Winter 1994, my junior year of high school, I got a car for my sixteenth birthday. It wasn't the car I wanted, but it got the job done. A 1987 Dodge Aries K. No single skill I have ever learned has brought me more joy, or more opportunities, than learning how to drive. It was life-changing.

I eagerly volunteered my car to take junior varsity baseball players to practice, and they all declined. I was nowhere near as cool as Johnny Edwards. Plus, the car had a loud rattling motor from something going on with the head gasket. It was perfectly fine to get me from A to B and gave me the right to no longer ride the school bus every morning. But it was not a car fit for junior-senior prom, which was fast approaching. I needed better wheels.

I begged and begged my father all winter to let me drive one of his Lincolns—just for that one night. He had a maroon 1989 Lincoln Continental, and it was perfection. It had power windows, power steering, leather seats, and a suspension that made you feel almost weightless. I won't even compare it to riding on a cloud because even a cloud would be too rough of a ride.

Later that week I came home to my father sitting in the living room, smiling.

"Let's go to the grocery store," he said. "You're driving."

Getting my learner's permit and then my driver's license brought me closer to my father than any other event in my life. In transit is when we actually talked—about any- and everything: girls, baseball, his speaking engagements. It was all so odd to me because I never really talked to my father at the house.

To be in the car with him just felt normal. He talked to me more like a man now. Once in a blue moon he would talk about my half siblings and stress that I needed to have a relationship with them, especially my younger half brothers. Knowing what I know now, my father knew he didn't have that much time left on earth and was simply sharing what he hoped for his children after he was gone. If there wasn't anything to discuss, then the silence was filled with talk radio or jazz.

Over the next few months, I essentially became my father's driver. If he had a speaking engagement, a pawnshop run, or a potential vehicle or camera purchase to inspect, I was his guy. On Saturday mornings, my father worked at Alabama State doing a radio show for their campus station. If I wasn't working, I drove my father to and from Montgomery. It was about an hour each way. I never told him this, but eventually I requested afternoon shifts just so I could get up to give him those rides in the morning. We would usually leave the house around 8 A.M. and be back in Birmingham by noon. I was thrilled, of course, because not only was I driving, but I was driving a car at seventy miles an hour. We talked a little here and there, but for the most part my father slept. Those times meant a lot to me because I knew in that moment that I was doing something for him. I felt needed, I felt wanted, and that wasn't a feeling I felt very often with my dad. I was a kid who just wanted to spend time with my father, and at that point in my life I didn't care what we did anymore, I was just thrilled to be there. The radio stayed locked to AM news channels. I guess he was listening with his eyes closed. His car, his rules. "None of that rap shit in here," he'd mumble before dozing off.

It's also possible that my father asked me for these rides simply because he was tired. I didn't realize it at the time, but his prostate cancer had returned with a vengeance. My father had been diagnosed with prostate cancer about fifteen years prior but had never shared that news with me. He might have shared his condition with my mother back in the '80s, but he offered her no updates after that. It wasn't until the spring of 1995, when it was obvious that the cancer was here to stay, that my father's illness became an omnipresent influence on his behavior, and the dynamics between him and me shifted for the worse. I learned most of what I now know about my father's illness after he died. We never discussed it at the time and my mother didn't bring it up.

All I knew as a fifteen-year-old was that my dad had cancer and it was bad. I didn't even know at the time that he only had a year left to live, or that he was skipping chemotherapy and had been doing so since the late '80s when he was first diagnosed. Maybe he'd taken a little chemo at that time, but I know for sure that he didn't later in life because he wanted the energy he had left to be used for working. So he opted for pain meds over radiation.

Like most men, my dad was extremely proud, and I don't think he relished the idea of needing to be driven around, but he loved having the opportunity to sleep more as he went from gig to gig. That was pretty much the bulk of our relationship for that spring of 1995.

That fall, I only knew that the cancer was out of control and that my father was getting ready to pass, because more and more people started coming by the house to talk to him. Each night, my father would field about two to three hours' worth of visitors.

When he was able to stay awake, we talked about a lot of different things in the car, but we never discussed his relationship with my mom very much. He never went into detail about what had happened between them, but whenever it came up, he was always quick to say, "I love you. You know I love you. I'm very proud of you. You are my bloodline." Those moments didn't happen often, so I never really knew how to process them. I just nodded and continued to drive.

I've never felt closer to my father than I did in 1995. But there were so many missed moments between us. I don't think he ever fully knew how to explain why he treated my mother the way he did, and I don't think I was prepared to ask the questions that would have pressed him for an answer. So instead, we sat in silence. I guess I didn't stress it because my mother had found her own rhythm and most of their fighting had subsided by the time I started high school anyway. My mom was done with law school and studying for the bar exam. Once she passed it, she would be a licensed attorney and be able to build the money she needed to plot her exit from the home. I figured asking questions would just stir things up anyway. Anytime I asked a question that hovered anywhere too close to their marriage, he accused me of being a spy for her or said that she put me up to asking that question. Best to let sleeping dogs lie.

One afternoon while we were riding together in the car, he mumbled under his breath reluctantly, "If you take it, you have to wash it and detail it and vacuum it. If you take care of my car, then I will allow you to go to your junior prom in the vehicle."

I was speechless. I couldn't believe he'd relented. I'd stopped asking about the prom months earlier. I rented a tux from Mr. Burch in Western Hills Mall, and when the night came, I scooped up my prom date in that maroon 1989 Lincoln Continental. I felt like a king in that Continental. It rode like a dream—wide body, even wider tires, beautiful suspension. I was so short I could barely see over the hood when I sat behind the wheel. Driving that car was like driving an cruise ship. But it was the perfect chariot—and a perfect night.

Sadly, the good vibes between my father and me began to subside. The more his cancer grew, the more our relationship soured. I can only assume that when you are in that kind of pain on a regular basis, it will alter your mood and maybe how you perceive situations. Suddenly, he was more irate than ever, snapping about little things.

Things at home were deteriorating. There was no love lost between my father and my mother, but he became even more blatant and open in his disrespect to her. Also, Valerie had died suddenly two or three years earlier, and her death continued to haunt my father. He loved her and missed her. He refused to stay in the home they had together after her death, and my two younger brothers were now across town being raised by their aunt and uncle. My father would rather be miserable than alone, so he was back to staying with me and my mom full time after Valerie died. Further compounding things at home was a new houseguest. A relative on my dad's side came to live with us for what I can only guess was an attempt to have a better relationship with my father. I've never sought out the details. To me, he was just another person in the long line of people coming by the house on a regular basis to be extra nice to my dad. Only this person spent the night.

The guest wasn't a fan of my mother, nor did he offer her much respect. But no one encouraged him to; he was just following my father's lead. Sometimes my father would walk around the house, snarling at my mother at random. "You need to get the fuck out of my house, bitch," he'd say. "I'm sick of you being here."

And of course, because this was my mother, I couldn't let my father talk to her any kind of way. I dared to stand up to him, which only made him more indignant toward me, because, in his eyes, he'd done so much for me. That summer of 1995, I dreaded going home. I begged for extra shifts at work and did everything I could to stay out of the house. Tensions in the house remained high. You'd have my father and his relative on one side and me and my mother on the other: rival nations with ballistic missiles locked on each other and their finger hovering over the button.

Then one day my father fired a shot.

I was lying fast asleep in my room on a Saturday morning when I heard my father thunder up the stairs. He never came upstairs unless I was in trouble, and he definitely shouldn't have been coming up the stairs with full-blown prostate cancer in his body. But he had a point to make. With every inch of strength left in his being he willed himself up those stairs, fueled completely on rage. He used his cane like a SWAT team battering ram and crashed my door open. His eyes were bulging out of his head, almost comically. You could see every blood vessel in his eyeballs.

"You ungrateful motherfucker! You ungrateful motherfucker!" he yelled. "You and your mother, I'm sick of y'all's shit. You wrecked my fucking car. You wrecked my fucking car!"

"Dad, I don't know what you're talking about," I said.

He raised his hand to hit me, then stopped himself. "I can't have anything in this goddamn house. Anything that's mine, you just fucking take and take and take. Go out there and look at my car, you motherfucker."

I got up, went downstairs, and went into the garage. As I walked around to the side where the '89 Continental was, I saw that the side paneling on the garage door was gone as if something had swiped it. As I crept around to the passenger side of the car, I could see the side-view mirror was gone and there was about a three-foot scrape on the side door.

Fuccccccckkkkk. Fuck fuck fuck fuck fuck fuck.

The car had been perfectly fine when I'd gone to bed, and my father had gotten up at 7 A.M., so that meant the scrape had happened sometime the previous night. I'd never snuck out of the house in my entire life.

But there my father stood, yelling at me for wrecking his car. I knew who'd done it. It was our new houseguest. That person knew that he'd done it. He knew he'd taken the car out that night and damaged it. But he had no interest in owning his mistake. He saw my father talking shit to me, to my face, and had already seen the way he'd talked about my mother, and he didn't say anything. I looked at the real culprit and he smirked. My father was giving me the same enraged look he'd given my mother when she'd slammed that baseball bat into the windshield of his Mercury Cougar.

I told him who I suspected did it. I knew it was our houseguest, but he wasn't trying to hear that.

He was done with me.

He was done with me.

Our relationship was never the same after that.

In a single night, every conversation my father and I had had in the car going back and forth to Montgomery meant nothing. That foundation had been wiped away, and he had nothing in his veins for me but resentment. He stopped asking me to drive him places after that.

For whatever beef my father had with my mother, he had always seen me as a neutral party. After the incident with the car, I was no longer neutral. He saw it as an act of disrespect, and disrespect equaled war. And in war you must choose a side. That house held no Switzerlands. We didn't talk much after that. He was getting sicker and I guess he didn't have a desire to. People would come to the house and visit and I would sit and try to be cordial, but it was all empty gestures. None of it was sincere. We were presenting to outsiders like we were a functioning father-son unit, but deep down we both knew the truth. The cancer visits were hard—having a front-row seat to people thanking a man and telling you stories about a side of him that you never really knew. It was the same man, but we were mourning two different people.

One night about a month before he died, I walked into the living room and my father was on the couch going through his usual routine: local news, international news, *Wheel of Fortune, Jeopardy!* I sat down near him and started watching the news. I didn't say anything to him. He didn't say anything to me. We sat there in silence watching television together.

About an hour into this, he gathered enough courage to ask me to make him a baked potato. I obliged. I got up, wrapped a potato in a soaking wet paper towel, threw it in the microwave, and boom, baked potato. I plated it, added some butter and sour cream, and brought the little food tray over to the couch and set it there. I returned to my original perch and continued to watch television in silence.

When *Jeopardy!* finished, my father mumbled, "You can come get this." I turned around and he was sliding the plate in my direction. He'd taken two, maybe three bites of the potato. His appetite was pretty much nonexistent at this point, and he was mostly drinking Ensures for nutrients. But for him to have eaten anything, I guess, was good.

As I came over to get the potato, my father looked me in the eyes and said, "I did okay, didn't I?" And I said, "Yes, you did the best you could." He smiled and patted me on the hand.

This would be the final conversation I had with my father. A few days later, my father was checked back into the hospital and then after that into hospice at the home of an older half brother who lived across town.

One morning in early October 1995, about a month after the potato conversation, my mom came into my room.

"You should really go and see your father this week."

"Why? He's just lying there. He's usually asleep, and when he's awake, he's yelling and cussing at somebody about something."

"You should go and see your father this week."

I asked her if she was going.

"No," she responded. "But you should."

So I hopped into my '87 Dodge and headed out to my older brother's house. When I arrived, there were a shit ton of people inside and cars all over the lawn. This was not like any of the visits at our house. My dad was in far worse condition than when I last saw him a month prior. What I walked into was basically a living funeral. My dad was in a hospital bed in my brother's living room, and he was not present. Cancer is fucking horrible and atrocious, and if they told you the truth about what happens in those final weeks, there would be far better regulations on carcinogens and the things we consume.

What I saw was terrible. What I heard was terrible. What I smelled was terrible. I won't even put it in this book.

A man so strong reduced to skin and bones. It was hard. What I saw still haunts me to this day. My father was not present with us in that room. He was already gone. His spirit left his body long before he died. I hate that the memory of the last time I saw him alive was that. It's seared into my mind. Certain smells can take me back to that moment. Certain sounds can bring me back to that moment. I wouldn't wish memories this vivid on my worst enemies. Every day that I live, I regret going to see my father that last time. My mother had made me do it. But she could not have known what had happened to him.

Older and wiser today, I have to give my older brother a great deal of credit. There aren't a lot of people who would willingly accept a front-row seat to the death of their parent. I'm sure that took an incredible toll. Still, I oddly envied my older half siblings. I've always felt that my older siblings got a better, more loving version of our father. Even if he wasn't perfect with them, I feel like they got enough affection from him to properly grieve him as he neared death. I was sad that my father died, but I don't think I ever truly grieved him.

A week after seeing him, we got the call that my father had passed. I sat with my mother and we talked about it for a second, then I hopped in my car and went to school. Business as usual. I think working and finding something to focus on when things are emotionally heavy is my go-to. I'm still slightly annoyed that I was denied this on the day my father passed. Word of his passing was all over television and radio, so by the time I got to school at 8:30, everyone was looking at me like "What the hell are you doing here?" It was a truly sad day in the city. My father was being mourned by everyone but me. I just wanted to go about my day.

The convenience of cancer is that it gives you time to mourn the person's death long before it comes. I think the difficult thing is watching someone be celebrated and exalted by all the people he touched while you sit in awe and have to come to grips with the fact that you never got that same experience with that person. It is hard to do that when you harbor so many conflicted feelings. It's even more difficult when the rest of the world reveres the person that you sometimes feel you got the short end of the stick on. Turns out the reason why my father watched so many different newscasts is because he was mentoring all of the various anchors and reporters and offering them critiques in weekly meetings. Over the decades I've heard so many stories of his love and benevolence and giving and sacrifice, and it's made me wonder if he was all out of love to give by the time he walked in the front door of our home. I was sad, but I don't think I ever truly grieved.

You feel cheated, then you feel furious—neither of which is an acceptable emotion to show the week of your father's funeral. I didn't know at the time that I was simply trying to cope. But the teachers clocked it. As was tradition at Ramsay High School at the time, when someone in our student body suffered through the death of an immediate family member, a teacher would go from class to class and collect money for that student's family. Coach Lawrence Logan was the driver's ed instructor and also my baseball coach. He walked into the homeroom hanging his head and announced to the class that my father had passed and that we were taking up money to send to Roy and his mother. As Coach Logan finished the sentence he looked up and saw me sitting there. All of my classmates turned around; none of them knew what to say. My presence was officially a distraction, so sometime around third period I was called into the principal's office and advised that I should go home and be with my mother. They just treated me like a kid that was in shock. I guess I was.

I didn't want to be at home and sit and think about this. I parked out in front of the TV and played my Sega Genesis videogame console all day, but that wasn't helping. Thankfully, the owner of the Subway I worked at did not respect child labor laws, so I worked double shifts Tuesday and Wednesday since I wasn't allowed to go to school. I logged in about twenty-four hours of work in those two days.

My father's funeral was three days later at the historic Sixteenth Street Baptist Church in downtown Birmingham. It was standing room only. It was a beautiful Thursday morning.

I was emotionally detached from the whole experience. It was interesting watching myself and all of my siblings grieve differently. The funeral was kind of a joyous occasion for me because it was the first time I had seen any of my classmates that week. Some of my best friends skipped school that day to attend my father's funeral. I've never forgotten that gesture.

After the funeral came the burial. That's where shit got weird. As we arrived at my father's grave, I noticed something peculiar next to the hole that had been dug for him: Valerie's grave. As it turned out, when Valerie had passed a few years earlier, my father hadn't purchased one burial plot. He'd purchased two. So there I stood next to my mom, my father's widow, as we laid him to rest next to the woman he loved. I always took it as one last fuck-you from him to her, and I hated that for her.

As the funeral ended and we all dispersed back to our vehicles, my older half sister Brenda came up to me with words of encouragement. No matter the situation, Brenda has a Bible verse etched in her memory, ready to be laid out on the table like an ace of spades. Of all of my siblings, she's the most optimistic. She's also the most spiritual and therefore the most forgiving. I don't think I've ever met anyone in my life who moves more intentionally with love and spirituality as her guide. Her objective in any tough conversation is to try to pour her spirit into your empty cup. In those days, Brenda was the type of person to start a sentence with "The scripture says," and end a sentence with "Lord willing." But I'll be honest with you, I wasn't trying to hear that shit that day.

I wasn't necessarily mad at my father that day—the anger would come years later—but I also wasn't going to let someone else's journey with my dad dictate how I should or should not feel in the moment. Still, it didn't stop her from trying,

"You know Daddy always loved you, and I know he wasn't always everything we needed him to be, but just remember he did the best he could," she said.

I stopped dead in my tracks.

What Brenda said hit me like a ton of motherfucking bricks. My father was never asking if he'd done okay with the potato. My father was asking me if he'd done okay raising me. I'd misunderstood the question.

He was never asking me about that stupid fucking baked potato. And not only had I misunderstood the question, I'd given him the wrong answer. I'd given him the opportunity to escape accountability, to escape having a conversation and simply explaining some things to me. I understood his greatness because everybody told me about his greatness. There was no one around to tell me about his flaws. My father had asked if he'd done an okay job raising me, and I'd said that he'd done the best he could. And even if that's what actually happened, the truth was deeper than that. I had more to say.

If I'm being honest, if I had been aware of what my father was really asking me, I don't know what I would've said. What I do know is that it could have been an opportunity to truly understand him. I don't think I ever really mourned my father that week. Because even after his death he still thumped us behind the ear.

When my dad passed, the IRS came for his house to fulfill his back tax debt. Turns out he hadn't paid federal taxes for a few decades.

At the time there was a prevailing thought among some people in the Black community that even though the Voting Rights Act was signed into law in 1965, the Black man's right to vote would expire in the year 2007. This ended up not being true, as it was certain provisions surrounding the process of voting that would expire, not the right to vote itself. Still, this urban legend was enough to cause my father to believe that the government did not deserve a penny of his income.

To which the IRS said, "Whatever, motherfucker, we'll just wait for you to die and then we'll kick your widow out of your house and sell it."

My mother had a great deal of legal savvy and knew just what paperwork to file, to drag out the process. Thanks, Bill Handel. She and I managed to scrape up enough money to pay the bills just long enough for me to graduate high school.

When they sent me home from school the day of his death I did not stay put at the house. I knew we would need money to supplement the income he was bringing in. I took his cameras and hid the really valuable ones in my car and in empty lockers at school. One by one that week I took them around and sold them off to all the collectors and pawnshops that he and I used to frequent. I also started working thirty hours a week, instead of the usual twenty that was legally allowed for a minor. My mother and I had a long conversation, and we agreed that she should cash in the prepaid college tuition money that she had been chipping into for the last decade. I don't know how much money it was, but it was enough to keep us afloat until I left for college freshman orientation the summer of 1996. The same day I left for Tallahassee, she surrendered the home to the IRS and moved into a modest two-bedroom apartment in the Birmingham neighborhood of Ensley.

The thing I remember most in the days after my father's death was how few of *his* friends came to our house to pay respects. They all gathered at my older brother's house or at other prearranged spots around town to celebrate his life. My father never demanded that people respect my mother though she was still his legal wife. So why would they respect her in his death. But in disrespecting her they disrespected me.

This made so many of their glowing comments about my father hard to swallow later in life. These people all over Birmingham who my father touched, who my father helped, spoke to me with such reverence about all the things he had done for them. I think most were too obtuse to even realize that they were speaking to the child of a woman who, as far as I was concerned, they had disrespected. I couldn't mourn my father properly because every week there was another financial fire to put out or someone in my face telling me the usual "let me know if you need anything I am always here for you."

Bullshit.

A few years ago, I was scrolling through a parenting book and came across this line: "Ask your children one thing they love about you and one thing that stresses them out about you."

When you were seven, son, I asked you this and you told me that you didn't like it when I yelled. You and I talked and worked through why I might be yelling. I wasn't necessarily defending the yelling. And what might be yelling, to you, could just be talking sternly as a parent to me. But I wanted to open the door for feedback between you and me.

I enjoy walking to school with you. Our walks aren't quite the same as the rides I took to Montgomery with my father, but I like them because they give me an opportunity to talk to you. The brain of a child is like a lottery ball hopper. There are a million questions rattling around in that brain, some simple and some extremely layered and complex, and you never know which question is going to come up during that walk to school. When your mother and I shifted to coparenting, you asked me once about our dynamic. "Why don't you live with us anymore?" you asked one day. Your mother and I sat you down to talk to you about what joint custody would look like and why, even though you were going to live between two houses, we'd remain one family.

My father's final lesson to me in many ways was the most important to parenting: Have an open line of communication and critique with your child. You're not perfect and sometimes the people who are closest to you are indeed the most qualified to tell you that, even if they're just seven years old. While I didn't get to say everything I wanted to say on the night of the baked potato, I am happy that my father knew that somewhere underneath all of that, I still loved him. There's a lot we could have communicated and probably gotten to the bottom of if I had been able to check in with him from time to time.

Kids don't know how to open that door of conversation on tough topics. It's on the parent to take that step, even if they're fearful of not liking what they're going to hear after they open it. Because I realize now that my father kept that door closed to me, I work hard to keep that door open for you.

CHAPTER 8

No Fear

When I opened the case and looked at it the first time, I was rendered speechless. It was beautiful. It was truly stunning. It was gold with a large turquoise stone in the center.

I, like many other high school students in the '90s, was duped into purchasing one of those stupid class rings. It would be a few more years before I conceded that jewelry wasn't my thing. But at the time, a class ring was *the* premier status symbol. Shoes were important to fitting into the status quo, as were jeans at that time. Having a car could elevate your status, but having a car *and* owning jewelry raised your status even more—especially if you were a senior.

To give you some more context, if you were a high school senior in 1996, it was understood that a few things were going to happen.

1. You were going to have sex at prom.
2. You were going to go on your class trip.
3. You were going to get a class ring.

I nailed two out of three on that list. My high school girlfriend was a saint so we didn't have sex, but I did get my class ring. And I did go on our senior class trip to Mexico where I did have sex. I guess that counts as all three, right?

The ring came from a company called Herrf Jones. They were the go-to company for priceless high school memorabilia that would mean absolutely nothing to you by the time you left college. They'd send a representative to the school and you'd get called out of class to go look at the big glossy catalog in the gym. The rep would talk to you in that same tone that the scammers in Vegas do when they're trying to sell you a timeshare.

As soon as you approached the table, he would offer a smile with way too much teeth, shake your hand firmly, and then say, "Son, I'm telling you this class ring is an investment that will pay you dividends for years to come."

You'd take the catalog home and flip through it, looking at all the design possibilities. A class ring was basically a charm bracelet for your finger. You could choose from an array of pictures and logos and symbols that all helped to tell the story of who you were in high school. And you could do it all for the low, low price of about five hundred fucking dollars. The ring I selected was around four hundred thirty-five dollars. I was a little cheap.

There were sports designs, arts and crafts, hobbies. You could put your state on the side of the ring. Pretty much whatever you wanted. And, of course, on the inside of the ring you could engrave your name and a stupid catchphrase. On one side of my ring, I opted for a baseball with "21" (my jersey number). On the other side, I put my zodiac sign. Because yep, what that's what I wanted people to know about me: I love baseball, and I am a Sagittarius. On the inside of the ring, I had them put the quote from my senior yearbook.

"Don't be afraid to take chances. No fear."

A few weeks later these $500 behemoths showed up at the

school. We seniors proudly walked around the school with these forty-pound barbells hanging from our hands. Some guys would even let their girlfriends wear them. Hip-hop had deemed jewelry a status symbol. It made you feel cool. My class ring was my prized possession. I worked extra shifts at the rehab hospital cafeteria, even if it meant working with Cocaine Mike, just to pay for it. I loved it.

And it almost got me killed.

■ ■ ■

Before I continue, I should say: I've had a gun pulled on me five times in my life.

Three times it was by the police, including on a couple of overly aggressive traffic stops where the cops deemed it necessary for me to toss my keys out the window and walk backward to their vehicle. Once, an arresting officer buried his 9mm Beretta deep into my rib cage, almost daring me to make a move. Cooler heads prevailed, thankfully, and I lived to tell the story.

The other two times were business deals that went south. My freshman year of college me and some buddies got into an argument with a bunch of Jamaican club owners who we believed were price gouging the cost of admission into their nightclub. The disagreement quickly boiled over into a full-blown shouting match ending with seven or eight Jamaicans pulling guns and machetes on me and my friends. We still ended up inside the club, laughing and hugging the Jamaicans hours later.

The last time I had a gun pulled on me would be years later in Dothan, Alabama, at a comedy show that was being run by a few drug dealers. They had taken the money from the tickets they sold from the show and purchased a brick of cocaine. They hoped to sell enough of the cocaine to make the money they needed to pay the comedians. When this bit did not pay off, they locked us in the green room before the show and made us promise to perform for free with the understanding that we would be sent our money via Western Union the following week.

When some of us refused to perform for free, a gun was drawn and laid on the table and we were asked to strongly reconsider our position. I was still a young comedian at the time, so I left it to the more senior comedians in the room to figure a way out of this predicament for us. The solution was that everyone would perform for free, and if any of us wanted to be paid in cocaine instead of cash, the drug dealers would be happy to do so. I agreed to these terms and then asked to go outside to make a phone call. When I got outside, I got in my car and sped away. The drug dealers called me all kinds of names on my voicemail and then called the radio station I was working at to curse me out the following morning on the air. They turned out to be pretty honest guys and the comedians who performed for free were not only paid the next week via Western Union, they were paid double.

I should have taken the cocaine.

But as terrified as I was in these moments, the most scared I've ever been was on a night when no gun was present. It was just me, some friends, and my ring that was engraved "No fear."

■ ■ ■

Everything that made you cool in high school immediately makes you uncool when you get to college. As I stepped onto the campus of Florida A&M University in the fall of 1996, I immediately went from being top dawg to being a puppy again. As a freshman, you tried to cosplay being a senior as quickly as you could. You needed more jewelry, you needed a car, you needed to live off campus—anything that could impress a woman in college. You needed to be rocking Tommy Hilfiger, Ralph Lauren, Cross Colours. The cost of being cool immediately tripled when you got to college.

You know what would not impress a woman in college? A Herff

Jones high school class ring. And you could leave that stupid senior letter varsity jacket in your hometown as well. All of a sudden, the class ring that I'd worked extra shifts delivering food to sick patients for was an obsolete chunk of metal. I banished it to the back of my jewelry drawer like that ugly watch your aunt bought you that you don't like but you wear whenever she comes around because you want her to *think* that you like it.

And that was where my $500 class ring sat for most of my time in college—in the back of my jewelry drawer next to my cufflinks and a few shitty watches. From time to time, I would pull my ring out and look at it. I never wanted to wear it, but I also refused to sell it. It still had sentimental value. It reminded me of a quieter time in my life. When I waited tables, however, I'd wear it. It was a useful conversation starter with customers.

I spent two years living on campus before my friends and I finally got our first off-campus apartment. Finally, we were able to drink and party without fear of noise complaints or some snitching dormitory RA banging on the door.

We lived in the Palms of Magnolia apartment complex right behind this very popular nightclub called The Moon. And because our apartment was walking distance from the hottest nightclub in Tallahassee, on Friday and Saturday nights we became the de facto staging area for friends who were looking for a safe place to underage drink and play a little PlayStation before hitting the club scene.

We were good guys, just testosterone-driven men who wanted to drink, get laid, and make good enough grades so that our parents wouldn't drive down to campus in the middle of the semester and embarrass us. We had a spacious townhome with three sizable bedrooms tucked away upstairs. On any given night, it wasn't uncommon to come home to find anywhere from eight to ten people there. Often the last person would not leave until 3:00 A.M. It all seemed perfectly normal to me, that was just the way things were.

One night, I came home to a stripper dancing in our living

room. She had been booked by a few friends that were visiting from out of town. This was not the way things normally were. As I stood there removing my apron from my restaurant job, I was trying to piece together what the hell was going on.

"Yeah, Wood. Come over here and get a lap dance, Wood. Come over here and get a lap dance!" my friends drunkenly screamed at me. They threw a few dollar bills at the woman to encourage her to move my way. She obliged. When she got close, we both winced at each other's odor at the same time.

"Ugh, nigga, you smell like a kitchen," she proclaimed as my friends laughed. Before I could respond, the smell from her aggressive smoker's breath hit my nostrils and stopped me dead in my tracks.

The gray hairs starting to sprout from the base of her scalp suggested she'd been at this awhile. I was too young to approximate age, but a gray hair to me at that time meant you had to be at least sixty years old. She was probably in her mid- to late thirties.

I won't say this woman was ugly. I'll just say that if you saw her in a strip club, you'd ask her to point you to where the strippers were. But nonetheless, here she was in our living room, butt-ass naked. She received money in exchange for being butt-ass naked. That pretty much meets all the criteria for being a stripper, I guess.

I've never really been a fan of stripping. It's just never done anything for me from an arousal standpoint. I've always viewed it as paying someone to give you blue balls. But after a full day of classes and another six hours in a restaurant serving strangers, I was perfectly fine with kicking back with a drink and watching a woman with creaking knees twirl her way around the living room as obnoxiously loud Luther Campbell music blared from our Aiwa stereo system.

About a half hour later she wrapped up and all of the boys chipped in whatever money they had to meet her flat rate. As she went upstairs to put her clothes back on, a wave of people made their way out the door to The Moon to enjoy the buzz from the cheap gas station liquor they'd been sipping on for the last two hours.

About twenty minutes later, the woman came back downstairs and mumbled something to the effect of "Which one of you schoolboy motherfuckers is going to take me back to my house?" We looked around and the only person in the room with a car was me. "I know y'all think I'm supposed to take her home 'cause she specifically said schoolboy. My GPA is at 2.4, so I know she's not talking about me," I joked.

Now, this wasn't my stripper. I hadn't hired her, so I didn't understand why it was my responsibility to take her back to her house. I insisted that she go up to The Moon and find the man who'd hired her and tell him to take her home. But what I considered to be a sensible suggestion only fueled her growing frustrations with us. She calmly repeated the terms of the verbal contract she had with my friends that hired her. "I ain't walking up to no Moon. One of y'all gon' take me home like you said you was." We quickly ran through our options. Cellphones were slowly becoming a thing, but not everyone had one in 1998, so there was no way to contact her ride. In Tallahassee the city buses stopped running around 10 P.M., and it was almost midnight. We offered to call her a cab, but she would only accept if we paid for it, and my roommates said no. And I held firm in my refusal to take her home.

"Miss lady, I don't even know who you are, I just got home. Look like you stranded until the bus start running in the morning, I don't know what to tell you," I said under a chuckle.

She slapped the table, sprang to her feet, and blurted, "You motherfuckers better take me back to my motherfucking house, or I'm going to call Lucius and there's going to be some motherfucking problems. And you motherfuckers don't want to see Lucius."

My roommates and I looked at each other in confusion. I had no idea who Lucius was, but I knew she wasn't bluffing. Gray hair and smoker's breath aside, she was still a Black woman. Everyone in that house was the product of a Black woman. And Black women all have the same posture when they're sick of your shit. This woman's "pissed-off" form was impeccable. No sense in letting her escalate this to the manager, God knows who Lucius was or what he'd do to us. I popped up and grabbed my keys. She and I hopped in my 1987 Dodge Aries and off we cruised into the Tallahassee night.

If you've never driven an adult dancer home after an hour of stripping for your teenage roommates, let me tell you, there's not a lot of exciting chitchat. "So you're a schoolboy, huh?" she mumbled between drags of her menthol. She didn't even ask for permission to smoke. But I guess at a certain age, do you need permission? I couldn't really put it together, but this woman did not feel like a stripper, at least not by trade.

The scuffs on her knees and ankles were akin to the abrasions that we'd accumulate on the streets of Clarksdale, Mississippi, from hours of two-hand touch football, which after a few possessions eventually became two-hand shove.

She was also very shifty in the car, nervous even. She clutched her purse far too tightly, if you ask me. I just figured it was drugs. She struck me as similar to some of the people I met in my time working at Subway in the Five Points South bar district of Birmingham—her behavior in my car fell well within that spectrum, so I wasn't nervous. I just thought it was odd. You made the money, you're getting a ride home, mission accomplished, right?

Thankfully our destination was only ten minutes away, so I didn't stress about having real, in-depth conversation. I let her drive the convo. We laughed about the various ways in which my friends were turned on by her. She said, "You college boys always want a girl to get butt-ass naked first. You need to understand the art of seduction. Let a woman seduce you. Let a woman know you are turned on by her. That turns her on. And then it makes her want to get butt-naked for you. But you college boys, y'all just horny. Horny, horny, horny."

She took a couple slow drags on her menthol and turned toward me. "It's a shame you missed out on the fun tonight," she said. "You want a private show?"

I explained that I was saving up for a major car repair and trying to work more shifts at Shoney's restaurant. To which she replied, "Pull over behind that Wendy's and I'll suck your dick for twenty dollars."

I don't think I've ever had a conversation take a sharper left turn in my life than I did in that moment. I immediately regretted my attempts at small talk with this woman. Also, twenty dollars felt dangerously cheap for a blowjob. You get what you pay for, and twenty dollars sounds like you're paying to get an STD.

My car chugged along as we approached her drop-off in a neighborhood called Frenchtown—a fairly rough area by Tallahassee standards. There was nothing there that I hadn't already seen before in Birmingham, so I wasn't nervous about the surroundings. It all looked and felt familiar. She declined to give me a specific address and instead had me drop her off at the McDonald's near Florida State University on Tennessee Street. We exchanged goodbyes, and then I busted a U-turn and went home.

At the house, I started my evening routine of taking a shower. Always when I got undressed, I took off my watch and put it in my watch drawer. This time, however, I noticed that my other watches were missing. I only had three watches in total, so initially I didn't think much of it. My roommates and I would sometimes wear one another's watches to create the illusion that we had a larger collection of jewelry than we actually did.

Then, as I opened the drawer even further, I noticed that a pair of cufflinks was gone. And also missing, my Herrf Jones class ring. That's when I knew for sure something was up. I sprinted downstairs and rang the alarm. I demanded that everyone in the house stop what they were doing right then and go to their rooms and check for their valuables. "She got us! She got us! Check ya shit! Go check ya shit!" I screamed like a drill sergeant. The boys sprang to their feet and all ran upstairs to check. Sure enough, everyone was missing something.

We held an emergency meeting in the living room about what to do.

How could this woman dare violate us? Who the fuck did she think she was to steal from us?

Everyone agreed. Looking back on this it's kind of funny because none of us had a gun, nor did we know anyone with a gun, but we needed to have the power of intimidation on our side when we got to where we were going. If it came down to it, I don't think anyone in my circle of friends at that time had it in them to strike a woman even if she did just steal from you, but the woman would not know that, and there was no way we were going to get our belongings back without some show of force. We needed weapons.

For some strange reason I still had my high school baseball bat. It was an Easton C-Core and I grabbed it. One of my other roommates grabbed a knife from the kitchen. We hopped in the Dodge Aries and sped back to Frenchtown to find this woman. Okay, well, maybe not sped, but we went as fast as we could without the engine in my car cutting out.

We did a lap around the McDonald's but did not see her. Not only did we not know where this woman was, but none of us knew her name because none of us had hired her. The guys who could answer that question were neatly tucked away inside a ten-dollars-a-head nightclub. Since this was 1998 and texting wasn't an option, trying to shake down those guys for information was only going to burn time we did not have. I figured we had a better shot of just snaking up and down the blocks of Frenchtown until we found this woman.

We parked the car blocks behind the McDonald's, deeper into Frenchtown, and got out on foot. Between the four of us, there were two weapons: a bat and a knife. Zero guns. Not even a pair of brass knuckles. We were schoolboys indeed.

We gave this woman's description to everyone we ran into and asked them if they'd seen her. Some of these people were winos and drunks, some were clearly sex workers, and none were very cooperative, but then again, considering the circumstances, how quick would you be to give the location of your friend to four teenagers who were holding a knife and a bat?

The logical side of my brain began to kick in and I realized that if she was a dancer, then maybe she was hired from a service. "Hey man, we just need the phone number of the company that set this up," I suggested as we swiftly walked up the block.

"Man, did she look like the type of motherfucker that has a phone? They didn't hire her from a service, they found her earlier tonight and asked her if she wanted to come dance," my friend replied.

"Wait a minute, you're telling me that you all brought a prostitute into our home!" I screamed.

"They're only prostitutes if you have sex with them. We brought a *dancer* home, now whether or not she moonlights doing other things is her business," said another one of my friends, who was offended that I would even suggest that he had to pay for sex.

"You did not bring a dancer home, you brought home a woman who *sometimes* has sex for money, but instead she decided to dance."

I could not believe what I was hearing. We were standing in the middle of the street holding weapons arguing the nuances of dancing versus sex work.

"You fucking morons thought that *sex worker* and *stripper* were interchangeable. That's not how the power of dance works," he said.

The one thing we knew for sure was that this woman answered

to a man named Lucius. So we started asking for him instead. Now it was time to escalate our complaint to a manager.

Almost nobody in Frenchtown would talk to us. They wouldn't even give us the dignity of answering the question at all. That we were college students was obvious from our attire and the way we enunciated our words. We were outsiders in a very dangerous world where we did not belong. At this point we had been walking block to block for about twenty minutes. We happened upon one of the people from earlier, one of the sex workers. This time we asked her if she knew Lucius. She tried to play dumb but stutter-stepped in her response. She was lying.

We loudly proclaimed, "We ain't leaving this fucking block until we find Lucius! Ain't none of y'all making no fucking money tonight!" But a bunch of schoolboys making threats didn't bother them at all.

A few minutes later, as we continued down the street, a car cruised up alongside us. There was a stillness to the occupants inside. The boys and I stormed over to this vehicle and immediately asked about the whereabouts of Lucius. Inside the vehicle were two men, Black, midfifties. I couldn't tell you much else about them, but their Afros definitely commanded attention. The man in the passenger seat for sure had lived a life. He had scabs and scars in very odd places.

"Hey, man, do you know Lucius?" I asked.

No reply.

"Hey. man, do you know Lucius? We are looking for Lucius."

Again, nothing.

My roommates were a little more hotheaded than me, and they escalated things.

"I know you hear me talking to you, motherfucker. Where the fuck is Lucius?"

I slapped my hand on the roof of his car to try to startle him. He didn't move. The longer he stayed silent, the more annoyed we became.

Finally, after what felt like forever, he pursed his lips and simply said two words: "Go home."

It was a bewildering response. "Fuck you, motherfucker. We are not going home. That fucking bitch stole my class ring and she's going to give it back to me."

The man again casually took a drag of the cigarette and again said, "Go home."

He continued, "You worried about what you lost, when you need to be thankful for what you still have. I am going to cruise this car down the street. I am gon' circle the block. When I come back, if y'all are still here stirring up shit, you're going to get what you were looking for."

It was very calm, but it was also very cold. Very ominous. The car cruised up the street, and the soft red glow of the brake lights slowly faded away from our faces as the car turned the corner.

There we stood in silence, trying to decide our next move. I was very upset. But really, when I thought about it, I was just embarrassed. Embarrassed that somebody had been able to get over on me. Embarrassed that I had been gullible. *I'm not a street guy,* I thought to myself, and I definitely was not interested in finding out what the man meant when he said, "You're going to get what you were looking for."

The grip on my Easton C-Core loosened a bit. I turned to the boys and said, "Let's go home." I can't speak for them, but I don't think they wanted any trouble either. We walked back up the block to my car and headed out. We didn't say much in the car. There wasn't much to be said. We had just gotten robbed by a stripper and punked by her supervisor. That deadness in his eyes was very real.

I've never felt more sure that death was close than on that night. And the man in the car never even made eye contact with us.

College is an interesting time because you essentially live your life in large emotional waves. Everything is either *great* or *devastating*. We assign large stakes to insignificant things. And things we should treat as significant we blow off as simple.

That night could have gone a million ways worse. And if that woman had wanted to, she could have screwed us over a million other ways. She could have stolen more. She could have lied and said she had a friend who wanted to dance for us and simply invited men over to put us all face down on the floor and rob us instead.

From that man that night I learned the importance of accepting the loss and taking time to extract the lesson from the loss.

Could you imagine dying or being forever crippled because you went behind a McDonald's to fight the fifty-year-old pimp of a thirty-eight-year-old sex worker and you're nineteen years old? I was walking around stomping and furious because a woman had stolen a piece of jewelry that informed everybody I was a Sagittarius who loved baseball. I didn't get a loss that night, I got a valuable lesson and lived to tell the tale. They say you can't put a price tag on an education. Well, I can—$435.

The guy from Herff Jones was correct. That class ring did pay in dividends that I'm still using to this day.

CHAPTER 9

Old Caterpillar

The main thing I remember about jail is that it was cold. Fucking cold. Every aspect of our justice system is cold. The police car, cold. Interrogation room, cold. Holding cell, cold. The actual jail cell, *fucking* cold. The blanket they gave you, at least in those days, was the thin bullshit blankets you still get on airplanes today. It did nothing to warm you up. Being cold is still the one thing that will drive me crazy. It immediately takes me back to the days of freezing in my father's house. The Leon County jail reminded me of my father, and not in a good way.

It was 1998, I was nineteen, and I had been in a Tallahassee jail since Wednesday night. This particular Wednesday fell on the week of Thanksgiving, which meant that there would be no arraignments and bail hearings until Friday.

I desperately needed to get out of jail. First, I needed to call the woman I was supposed to take to the new Will Smith movie, *Enemy of the State,* the night I was arrested, so that I could apologize. It was only our second date, but to ghost someone for two days straight is for sure a dick move.

The second thing I needed to do was call Shoney's restaurant and see if I still had a job. I'd been scheduled to work both days I was locked up, and missing a shift as a restaurant server on Thanksgiving Day was like not showing up for your shift at Best Buy on Black Friday. But when you're facing a five-year federal prison sentence, calling your shift leader to tell them that you're not going to be present to roll silverware wasn't exactly a priority.

As bad as some parts of my neighborhood were, I did not really see a lot of crime firsthand. But the one crime I witnessed more than anything else was shoplifting. My dad and I would be in line at Piggly Wiggly and, sure enough, some guy would casually walk past the cash registers. The walk would turn into a sprint as various steaks and fish fillets fell from his waistline.

Sometimes he got away, sometimes he didn't. I got bold enough one day in the fourth grade to steal a pack of Fruit Stripe gum from that Piggly Wiggly. My heart almost jumped through my chest. That successful attempt gave way to me trying to steal a toy space shuttle from the toy store in Century Plaza Mall the following year. As I tried to walk out of the store, the cashier sternly said between her gritted teeth, "Put it back."

The moment with the space shuttle concluded my life of crime until I got to college in the fall of 1996. These were the early days of paying for gasoline at the pump instead of going into the actual store. At the time, the receipt that came out of the pump had on it not only what you paid but also your entire credit card number, the expiration date, and your full name.

It just so happened that one day, when I stopped for gas on my drive back to campus, the person who'd gotten gas before me had neglected to tear their receipt off the pump. So when I got my receipt, their receipt was attached to mine, with a complete credit card number.

Jackpot.

Just to see if it would work, I ordered a few pizzas that night using the credit card number I'd found, with the intent of selling them in the dorms for two dollars a slice during *Monday Night Football.* You could order pizzas with a credit card over the phone as long as you showed the actual physical credit card when the driver arrived.

It was a perfect plan. In those days, very few places delivered pizzas to Florida A&M. We were in a part of town where there had been numerous robberies of pizza men.

The few pizza places that would deliver to campus made one request, that we meet their driver at a well-lit intersection designated as a pickup spot. Because of our neighborhood's reputation, when the white pizza man showed up, he was clearly nervous—shaking even.

Racism has its upsides.

If you are a pizza delivery driver and you are already assuming you might get robbed, then odds are you are also assuming that you are not getting a tip. No matter who we ordered from, the drivers were all the same. They all had the same nervous shake when they got out the car. Head on a swivel the entire time.

Before the driver could nervously say anything, I'd cut him off with my patented two-hit combo. First, I'd hit him with a quick "Hey, man, can you break a ten so that I can tip?" Shocked that a couple of Black seventeen-year-olds cared enough to tip, the driver would scramble to look through his pouch and I'd hit him with the second hit of the combo, "You know what, man, just keep the whole ten."

In under ten seconds I have subverted two stereotypes about Black people. One, I did not rob him and two, I tipped him. The kindness was enough to make the delivery driver forget all of his own protocols, including the one about asking me to show the physical credit card. The few that did ask for the card found my "I left my card at the dorm across campus" lie more than adequate, especially after a ten-dollar tip. No reasonable white person was going to sit on the edge of the hood with a pocket full of cash while they waited for a guy to make a fifteen-minute trek to get a credit card.

So for ten dollars I was handed about fifty dollars in pizzas, which would bring me about eighty dollars in cash. Minus the initial tip, I was up seventy dollars, I had zero overhead, and it took me less than an hour to sell all the pizzas.

That card number worked for a few more weeks before I lucked upon a restaurant that kept credit card receipts in an open stack by the register. Like the receipts at the gas pump, all the pertinent information was printed on the receipt. Jackpot. I'd swing by there once or twice a month and grab a good handful when the cashier wasn't looking and be set with new card numbers for the following weeks.

This was the general flow of my grifting until I took a work study as a mail sorter in the campus post office for some extra money. That's what was so nice about stealing. I was able to alleviate pressure on my mom. I could hear the relief in her voice when she knew I didn't need anything.

Years later in therapy, I would figure out that my stealing hadn't really been driven by the adrenaline rush of doing something and getting away with it. I'd simply wanted my mom to not have to worry about me. I'd known that if I could support myself—just as I had with my moneymaking schemes as a kid—she'd never have to call her friends for cash anymore. I was as free in Tallahassee as I was in Birmingham when I raked that woman's leaves for fifteen dollars.

It started out simple. In the '90s, most credit cards that were mailed to you were already activated. There was no need to call an 800 number or go to a website to start using the card. With this in mind, I quickly learned which envelopes contained credit cards. Most credit card companies are based in Delaware, and most envelopes coming from there were credit cards. Charlotte, North Carolina, was a huge banking hub. So cards coming from there were usually debit cards. I never touched debit cards. There was something heinous about stealing money from a student's account. In my mind it felt "better" to take from the banks. If I opened an envelope and it turned out to be a debit card instead of a credit card, I'd reseal it, stamp it as "damaged in transit," and still deliver it to the student's post office box. I would take those cards and order food to sell on campus, and sometimes I would go to the mall and buy clothes to sell on campus. Selling clothing opened me up to a different clientele than the usual teenager craving a pepperoni pizza. I met a lot of people in high places and very low places as well. One day it could be a drug dealer who wanted cheap clothes, the next an elected official who wanted a cheap suit. But business was business and I enjoyed being needed and appreciated. It was the first time I'd ever felt that.

I even broke down one week and got myself a nice pair of all-black Air Jordan 13s, the first substantial purchase I'd ever made for myself. Still, using hard-copy credit cards in the real world was much riskier than conducting over-the-phone transactions.

The biggest mistake I made in that stretch was using a credit card at a department store. I knew the cashier, so she allowed the transaction to go through even though her system flagged it as potential fraud. By the late '90s, credit card companies were starting to catch up with the fraudsters, so sometimes you needed a cashier who was in on the scam or just plain lazy and inattentive.

It took a few hours, but loss prevention at her store eventually put it all together and Tallahassee police were at my door. They scooped me up, but because I was nineteen and it was my first arrest, I was out of jail in under two hours on my own recognizance.

I got away that night, but deep down I knew that once they figured out the card I had used was addressed to the post office where I worked, they'd come for me again on a mail theft charge.

And indeed they came. I just never thought they would come the day before Thanksgiving, and to make matters worse they came before my date with that gorgeous woman, Melissa. This time, I was prepared. These cops were nice though. They let me pick which pair of shoes I wanted to wear to jail. I picked my Jordan 13s. Because you know what they say, if you're headed to an arraignment, be arraigned in style.

Court isn't a fun place, but it's warmer than jail, so I welcomed the journey to the courthouse that Friday morning for my arraignment. It would be a simple endeavor. The officers would trot me out in front of the judge and I'd stand there trying to look as innocent as possible. The judge would read off my charges and decide whether I'd get bail—and if so, what it should be—or whether I'd remain locked up until my trial months later.

Because I was in federal custody, I was being transported from the county jail to the federal courthouse by two U.S. marshals. I don't remember the first marshal that well, but I'll never forget the second one. He was one of those old-school white guys. He looked like the villain in every civil rights film set in the 1950s. On a good day he would get cast as the mean but repentant father in a made-for-TV race relations movie. This man could burn a hole through your head with his eyes. Gray and brown hair collected in heavy patches above both eyes and formed thick, caterpillar-like eyebrows.

His eyebrows were huge, like comically huge. Most eyebrows are flush against a person's forehead. His were almost a quarter inch off his face, like some sort of miniature Afro for his eyes. He wore regular slacks like every other federal agent, but for whatever reason, he wore old-school 1940s suspenders. His pants were hitched up high and I knew he meant business. Old Caterpillar got in the van and immediately blurted out, "No fucking talking in my van."

You've got to be a special kind of asshole to get in a car where no one is talking and the first order you bark is for no one to talk. He looked through the files and did a roll call to make sure they had all of the prisoners who were set to go to court that day. He got to my case and took a long look at it. Old Caterpillar looked at me and said, "I already know what's going to happen to a nigger like you."

My father definitely had his flaws as a man, but if there was one thing he had fully prepared me for, it was discrimination and how to not let someone who hated me affect me. But Old Caterpillar's words were still jarring. One of the advantages of growing up in a city as predominantly Black as Birmingham was that unless I was outside the city limits in the rural parts of Jefferson County somewhere, I didn't encounter racism this blunt and blatant.

Sure, when I'd been a food delivery driver delivering steaks to the affluent Birmingham suburbs, I'd been subject to some harassment by the police that patrolled those elite communities. Driving around in a raggedy-ass Dodge Aries gave the cops plenty of probable cause to say they observed some sort of mechanical infraction on the car. The cops would pull me over, but they'd see the hot insulated food bag in the back seat and send me on my way. Sometimes they'd even check the address on the receipt and help me find the street. God forbid I get to someone's house with a room temperature rib eye steak. My guess is that if the traffic stop had gotten too long and we'd informed some rich person why their food was cold, the cops might have found themselves on desk duty.

"Sorry I was late, ma'am, but the police officers you paid with your tax money were harassing me and that's why your dinner was ruined."

Blatant racists also popped up sometimes when my high school baseball team would play a white school from outside the city limits. They'd get brave and mumble "nigger" at us as they rounded first base. They always seemed to say it at a volume just below what the umpires were capable of hearing, oddly enough.

But this type of behavior did not shake us. We'd simply go back in the dugout and report the infraction to our pitcher. And the next inning the racist got a fastball to the ribs. Or, if there was a racist on the other team, and they made it to my home at first base, I would call for a ridiculous number of pickoff throws. When the player would dive back to the base, I would slap him abnormally hard in the earhole of his helmet. It doesn't seem like that horrible of a thing to do to someone, but if you hit someone in the earhole of their helmet over and over, and over, and over, and over and over again, they lose equilibrium and become disoriented. The white kids weren't dumb. They knew we were fucking with them. Whenever they made eye contact with us, we'd smirk.

Still, I don't recall a single game where we left infuriated or sad because of blatant racism we encountered on the field. We dealt with it on the spot and kept it moving. I don't think we ever told our coach. We never told our parents. I surely didn't tell mine. They were both from an era when a traffic stop meant imminent death, and Jackie Robinson had dealt with far worse. I knew how to cope with racism's blows. But this shit in the U.S. marshals' transport van was a direct hit. It's the type of racism you've always heard about but never experienced.

The transport van bopped and bounced down the Tallahassee streets as Old Caterpillar said "nigger" as hard and as loud and as often as he could, hoping that one of us in custody would react. He locked in on me.

"Let me tell you what's going to happen, nigger," he drooled. "You are going to go in there and look at that judge and that judge is going to send you right back to me, and we're going to come right back in this van and I'm going to take you right back to that fucking jail with all the other niggers, and that's where you'll be until your trial. When you get in that courtroom, don't you say a fucking word, and if you do say a fucking word, you're going to be in a world of shit with me, nigger. Do you understand me, boy?"

Refusing to give him the satisfaction of an answer, I just stared.

"Yeah, you hear me, nigger," he said. "I can tell."

I'm not sure if he thought he was making my day any worse, but at this point I was numb to everything. I didn't have any money for bail, and I still hadn't called my mom to tell her where I was, and that was a far scarier fate than being called nigger by bizarro Andy Griffith.

We arrived at the federal courthouse and one by one were shackled and escorted inside. The way Old Caterpillar had presented the run of show, it appeared that I was already fucked.

Every teenage child should be taken to see an arraignment. It should be part of civics education. Our culture has all of these silly television shows where they take young people to jail to meet inmates who'll give them "tough talk" and "tell it like it is" and "scare them straight." I guarantee you an arraignment will do the job twice as fast.

Being arrested is a bit of an out-of-body experience—you're not thinking clearly. But by the time you're arraigned, you've had time to think about the consequences of your actions. Put it this way: When a police officer slaps the handcuffs on you, and you get shoved in the back seat of that police car, you know you are fucked. An arraignment is where you are told precisely how fucked you are and how much it might cost to unfuck yourself.

This is where the most hardened people transform into horrified defendants. You can see it happen literally in front of you. An arraignment is where you are read your charges, you enter a plea of guilty or not guilty, and then if the judge sees fit, bail is set. It's like watching someone get on a roller coaster and they have a stoic game face until the attendant clicks that neck brace over their head and it locks in. Then, as the roller coaster starts clinking out of the station and up the hill, you can see their game face slip as the fear takes over.

This is what it is like to watch people who really do not want to be in jail being told they have to stay in jail until their trial.

We walked into the courthouse, single file, with the other defendants. The chains in our handcuffs clanked as if we were an old Southern chain gang. Old Caterpillar walked alongside us like a southern plantation owner on his imaginary horse.

"You better make sure when you get up there that you shut your fucking mouth. Do you understand?" he reminded us. No one replied.

The four of us all sat in the back of the room, and one by one we were unshackled and summoned down front to face the judge. We didn't talk too much.

The first guy in our group walked down to the front. Black guy around my age. He was pleading with the judge to make bail so that he could take his final exams, which were the week after Thanksgiving. He was set to graduate from Florida A&M in two weeks.

"Your Honor, I'm only asking for the opportunity to be allowed to post bail so that I can get my college degree. I'm the first in my family to go to college an—"

"Bail denied," said the judge. The gavel banged and that man hadn't even finished his plea. He collapsed to his knees.

I don't remember what he was being charged with, but it was nothing egregious. There were no murderers or sex offenders or carjackers in our lot. Most everybody was in for things like drugs, theft, and burglary. It seemed to me that allowing the man to be out on bail for a few weeks so he could get his degree before going to jail was a perfectly fair proposition.

As the bailiff dragged him out of the courtroom and into the bowels of the criminal justice system, the man wailed at the top of his lungs. He begged, he pleaded. It's a sound I will never forget.

Old Caterpillar smiled as he unshackled the next pig for the slaughter. The second guy headed up front to the legal guillotine. He said nothing, same game.

"No bail," the judge said.

Then it was the third guy's turn. Just as Caterpillar had instructed, he said nothing. The judge read his charges. The clerk read the recommended sentencing guidelines and made a recommendation of no bail.

"No bail," the judge said. "You will be remanded into federal custody until your trial." This guy trembled a bit.

Then it was my turn. I made my way to the front of the court-room, walking side by side with Old Caterpillar, who held my arm unreasonably tight and offered me up like a father presenting his daughter for marriage. The judge read my charges of mail theft, and the clerk read my previous charges for the credit card fraud. They asked me if I had retained counsel. I had not, so they put me in the system for a court-appointed attorney. The judge then asked the prosecution for their bail recommendation.

"Considering this gentleman's priors and his continued inability to obey the law," they replied, "we believe it is in the best interest of the court that he remain in federal custody until trial next year."

Next year? Before the judge could even bang the gavel, I spoke.

"Your Honor, could I say something?"

The fact that I even opened my mouth had Old Caterpillar *fuming*! He clinched my arm even tighter, cutting off the blood flow into my hand and forearm. But the one thing my parents had always given me was the freedom to speak up for myself. Even if my fate was still to be grounded, my parents heard me out. That court-room might as well have been the kitchen table in my father's house. It might as well have been my room on the night my mom found the Laffy Taffys in the trash. I was going to speak my piece.

The judge obliged me, and in about thirty seconds, I explained that this arrest was a follow-up to a previous investigation and that no new crime had been committed. So to suggest that I was still out committing crimes after getting arrested the first time was not fac-tually accurate. I was currently enrolled in college. My grades were decent. I was gainfully employed and could provide proof of em-ployment and residence. And the fact that I was an out-of-state stu-dent paying this tuition meant I wasn't a flight risk because I actually valued my education that I was already being overcharged for. Why pay all this money for classes if I'm going to not finish them?

The judge thought about it for a second and opted to let me go on a suspended $25,000 bond. This meant I could get out of jail without paying a dime, but if I missed a single court appearance I would owe the $25,000 in full, not the "$2,500, pay 10 percent" nonsense. He banged his gavel, and that was that. I was a free man. Caterpillar was fucking *livid*. That motherfucker damn near fainted.

Sitting with my mother in the car every morning listening to those law tapes finally did me some good. Thank you, Bill Handel.

As I turned from the judge to go back to my seat, I finally looked at Caterpillar for the first time, and I smirked. You could see the steam coming from his eyeballs. You would've thought I'd gotten his daughter *and* his wife pregnant. He slowly let go of my upper arm and the blood flow victoriously returned to my hand.

Caterpillar escorted me personally to the processing area where I did my paperwork to leave. He was exhaling so hard, snot was coming out of his nose with every breath.

"Sooner or later, you dumb nigger, you'll be back," he said. "And when you do, goddamn it, I'm going to be waiting on you."

The fury in his eyes was unforgettable. He had to personally un-handcuff me. It was glorious. I stepped out into the cool Tallahassee afternoon that Friday with a huge smile on my face and the refreshing breeze of freedom gliding across my skin. I headed straight to a pay phone to make two calls. First I called Melissa to see if she wanted to reschedule our movie date. She did not. Next I called Shoney's to see if I still had a job. I did not. I had no girl, I had no job, I had no friends, and according to my lawyer I was going to be headed to prison in about six months. So I did what any normal depressed nineteen-year-old would have done in that situation. I started doing stand-up comedy.

■ ■ ■

The next two years or so after that day, I had a lot of things fall my way. The only charge I was sentenced on was the mail theft charge because it was federal. Everything else was dropped. And in spite of facing five years in prison for the mail theft charge, in June 1999 I was instead given five years of probation. To this day, I don't entirely know why. I do know that a lot of people from my past wrote favorable letters to the prosecutor asking them to be lenient, including my high school baseball coach, Lawrence Logan, and the assistant dean of my journalism department, Dr. James Hawkins. Even my own lawyer told me I should have gotten at least two years in prison. He was as confused as I was at the sentencing.

My probation would eventually be dissolved after three years because of good behavior. I was hyperfocused on turning my future around and beginning my journey as a touring stand-up comedian. Along with that focus, I was assigned to a federal probation officer who saw my vision of what I was trying to accomplish. At every turn, he offered me support so that my federal supervision never got in the way of pursuing my dreams. I was very fortunate. It's like when I watch nature documentaries and see an antelope in the death grip of a lion, but for whatever reason on that day, the antelope wiggles away.

I'd gotten a job waiting tables at Golden Corral, which also happened to be the perfect testing ground for new material. My theory as a server was always if I can make you feel good then you are more likely to tip me. This meant figuring out ways to connect with people of all ages and races and walks of life.

Over time I figured out there are four connectors between all people: food, entertainment, love, and employment. No matter who you are from age eight to eighty, you love at least one thing in one of those four categories. Generally speaking, if you can get someone talking about one of those four connectors, then they will become happier in that moment. This theory would eventually become the basis of the joke structure that I use to this day when I'm attempting to quickly unify a room at the beginning of a comedy set.

It also works on large parties at restaurants.

"Roy, you got an eight-top over there," my supervisor said one day. "Don't you see them?"

"I got them," I said.

Because I was trying to decide which joke in my arsenal to hit people with first, I always looked at a table as I approached it. And as I walked up to this table, I realized it was a table full of police officers.

This was a layup.

Cops hate firefighters. Firefighters hate cops. Paramedics hate both. The army hates the navy and everybody hates federal agents. As far as I could tell, these beefs were rooted in each group thinking they were tougher than the other. Cops dodge bullets, but firefighters breathe smoke. Which is worse? It's debatable. And debate they did. I'd just slander firefighters a little bit, and I'd be in these guys' good graces immediately.

As I got closer to the table, I noticed the badges and realized I was serving U.S. marshals.

Suddenly, I heard a familiar voice. I turned around and there he was, Old Caterpillar. I almost froze, but a customer is a customer. For the next hour, I served this table full of federal agents the same as I would anyone else. I was kind, I was polite, and I said all of the right things. But every time I looked at Caterpillar, I was curious if he would remember me. The more he didn't notice me, the more I dropped hints, the more I gave him my patented smirk from the courthouse. Crickets.

I think I wanted him to recognize me because I wanted him to see that I was doing well, that I wasn't in prison. I wanted him to realize that people can change, grow, and be better. I wanted him to ask me how I'd been doing since then so I could tell him about my comedy journey. Finally, he looked at me. "More sweet tea, please, sir."

I don't know why him not recognizing me fucked with me so much. Maybe it's because that day was the day I finally understood how disposable Black people are to racists. It's one thing to be prepared for it after witnessing years of my father's rhetoric on TV and radio, but to feel it for yourself is different—affirming in a way. Good tippers, though, those U.S. marshals, a 25 percent tip. Way better than the Leon County Sheriff's Department, 15 percent. Cheapskates.

Son, people who have already shown that they don't give a fuck about you will never give a fuck about you, and your success in spite of their wrong assumptions about you is probably not going to change their opinion of you. Your growth is for you and you alone. So what if other people don't notice it.

I can't imagine saying the things he said to somebody and not forever walking around with my hand on my pistol and one eye looking over my shoulder. If he'd say that to me when I was already in custody, what the hell was he saying and doing to suspects that he'd arrested? What the hell was he doing when there were no other witnesses around? Lucius had been right the whole time. You take the loss, you get the lesson, and you move on. But this idea of someone giving you a pat on the head and telling you, "Good job, boy," is completely unrealistic. Lower your expectations. Make yourself better for you.

Old Caterpillar died a few years after that. The local newspaper, the *Tallahassee Democrat,* gave him a nice write-up, and he was heralded for his decades of service to his community. I'm sure in between calling Black people niggers on the transport van he probably did some good police work and was clearly admired by his peers. Maybe he survived a shootout or resuscitated a puppy or stopped a bank robbery. I'm sure there are some good things in his file. But still, when I read the article announcing his passing, I smirked.

CHAPTER 10

Lessons of the Golden Corral

've had a lot of jobs in my life, but serving at Golden Corral was the most important job I've ever had.

In the wake of my legal troubles, I desperately needed a lifeline. It showed up in the form of Golden Corral, a large family buffet–style restaurant with a big staff, decent hours, and a need for young workers. I started working there in 1998, about a month after my Thanksgiving-week arrest. I figured Golden Corral would just be a quick cash grab to pay rent and keep my life afloat while I traveled around doing open-mic comedy in the South. It ended up being so much more.

From the start, I loved the range of people I met there. Our educations and backgrounds were as diverse as our ages. Some of us were college educated, and some of us were dropouts. Some of us were there because we wanted a career in hospitality, and some of us were just transient.

We all answered to Miss Darlene. She was the senior shift leader and one of the most respected people in the building. She ran the front of the house and generally kept order, which wasn't an easy job. Every restaurant is split into two factions, the front of the house and the back of the house, and each side thinks the other one is keeping them from doing their job.

The back of the house would always complain that the servers were giving people too many plates, causing them to get too much food that they weren't eating, thus wasting the food, thus requiring the back of the house to cook more food. Meanwhile, the servers would argue that there was never enough of the food people wanted, so they had to get them some plates to stock up on food for their tables when that food actually appeared on the hot bar.

Or sometimes food orders would be in the window too long, which would make the back of the house annoyed because the food was getting cold, and if the food was cold, the first thing the customer was going to do would be to send it back and then you'd have a recook. There was nothing the back of the house hated more than a recook, especially if chef Mike Lou was on the grill.

Mike Lou didn't play with people. "What do you mean they don't like the steak?" he would snap at us. "I cooked the steak exactly the way that bitch wanted it cooked. I tell you what, next time I'm going to go out there and talk to that bitch and see what the fuck the problem is." Mike Lou was an artist. And if a customer sent a steak back to be recooked, he took it as an insult to his artistry. He had to know exactly what was wrong with his art. It could be a table full of Little Leaguers or a table full of U.S. marshals. Either way, Mike Lou was going to get to the bottom of it. He was a bold man. If only he were as smart as he was bold.

Mike Lou once threw a fish fry at his house and invited everyone from work. At one point, he went to the freezer to get more fish to keep the party going. He was so drunk that he completely forgot that the fish he was serving everyone was fish he'd stolen from Golden Corral. Suddenly, he was walking through a party full of Golden Corral employees holding a box that blatantly said "Golden

Corral catfish" on the side. Even so, I don't think he was fired for this, maybe just suspended or forced to pay for the product. If you're good at what you do, the rules don't apply.

It was just a bunch of merry men at Golden Corral. RJ was always charming and funny. He was important to the front of the house because he was the one server who had the respect of everyone in the back of the house. If there was ever any tension between the two, his charm and humor could defuse it. There was Simon. He was from Africa. I can't remember which country, but it was for sure one of those African nations where you feel comfortable talking down to Americans. He didn't crack a lot of jokes or hang with us that much; Simon just wanted to get his money and go home. However, he would turn into a fucking psychopath if he felt that you did not tip him well. A bad tipper would usually wait until the server went to the dish room and use that as an opportunity to sneak out of the restaurant. Simon would get the vibes that someone was going to stiff him on his tip, so he would lay a trap.

Simon would act like he was going to the dish room, then double back to the dessert bar and hide behind the ice cream machine, secretly looking at the customers and waiting for them to leave. When the customers got up, he would swing past the table. If he didn't like the tip, he would politely follow the customer to the parking lot and demand to be told to his face what exactly was wrong with his service. I don't know what made him think that this type of behavior was acceptable, especially in an open-carry state like Florida, but he did it on a regular basis.

The rest of the servers would gather at the window and watch the conflict unfold. Our jaws would drop when Simon not only was *not shot* but was given *more money* by the people he confronted.

There wasn't a single person in that Golden Corral who did not take their job seriously. It's also the only job I've worked where no one was nervous when the owner came, because we all knew we had our shit together. You weren't going to come in there and slack, because if you didn't pull your weight it would reflect on other people. This team would've taken Cocaine Mike out back and beaten the shit out of him for playing basketball on the clock and Mike Lou would've snorted his cocaine.

There was Mr. Willie. Mr. Willie was a retiree who worked only on Saturdays and Sundays to make omelets when we had a breakfast bar. During the breakfast bar, the person making the omelets was the single most important person in the building. He was like the lead singer of the group. And Mr. Willie knew he was the star. He was charismatic and cracked jokes with people, he dressed good and smelled good, he took pride in his work. He didn't do food prep, he didn't wash dishes, he literally would walk in and start working. I don't even think he ever clocked in. Like a surgeon arriving in the operating room to work on his patient, he had all of the tools that made him great at his disposal and waiting for him upon his arrival to the omelet station. Mr. Willie was a military veteran who spoke about war in ways so horrific that it made me very content in my choice to abandon the army ROTC scholarship I had been offered coming out of high school. You could tell he was someone who woke up every day and made the choice to enjoy life, and you could see it on his face.

And then there was Adolfo. Adolfo was meticulously groomed. His uniform was spotless and damn near tailored. The cuffs of his never-faded black work pants fell perfectly, gently brushing the top of his shoelaces. His work shirt was always freshly pressed. He even had the foresight to roll up the sleeves on his work shirt to accentuate his muscular biceps. The collar was stiff, and you could tell it had just a splash of starch or some collar stays inserted. His hair was always moisturized and he had a perfectly lined up mini-Afro. If you were a woman, he seemed like the kind of guy who wouldn't try to have sex with you on the first date. And if you were a guy, he seemed like the kind of dude that if he took all your money in a poker game, he'd still give you a little bit of it back to get a tank of gas. He was kind and suave, but not in a flirtatious way. It's just who he was. It was like if Will Smith's Mike Lowrey character from the *Bad Boys* franchise was a suave waiter instead of a police officer.

Marlon and Shod ran the back of the house. Shod had the most jokes and was also the resident DJ for the store after the customers left. Shod would crank the rap music so loud you felt like you were working in the dining room of a strip club in Miami. We cracked jokes and talked about life and love, but, most important, everybody fucking worked.

There was Eugene. He was a new father. He operated with a different sense of responsibility than all of us. He definitely loved his kid, and his girlfriend would bring his son by often to see Daddy at work. Between tables, Eugene would sit and talk with his son. There's something great about a child seeing their father make an honest day's living. I think it's an underrated part of child rearing.

Dads, retirees, playboys, angry immigrants, war vets, and me. Of course, droves of women worked there and made sure the store was a well-run machine, but socially I tended to gravitate toward the men. They provided me something I had not had up until that point in my life: a sense of morality and values.

Everywhere I turned at Golden Corral, there was a man offering me wisdom. But the boys in the dish room were the stars of the show, especially one boy we'll call Big Mixx. Big Mixx was either a young-looking thirty-five or a rough-looking twenty-five. Hard to tell. He was a classic Florida boy, gold teeth, some dreadlocks. He didn't laugh a lot, didn't talk a lot. He was a man moving with purpose.

No matter how fast you moved, you weren't bringing Mixx "his dishes" fast enough. He'd jam you up in the dish room like a high school football coach taking a private moment with a player who was underperforming on the field. "Hey, little motherfucker, you better bring me my goddamn dishes. I see you out here talking and flirting with these hoes. You need to be going around here bringing me my goddamn dishes. If you do the work, the pussy gon' come to you."

On a slow day Mixx would prowl the dining room looking for dirty dishes on tables. He contended that the servers were being lazy and not bringing the dishes fast enough, so he would do it him-fucking-self, he said. He would snake through the tables like a linebacker looking for a wide receiver to hit. As soon as a customer laid down a dish, Mixx would pounce.

Imagine you have someone as smooth as Adolfo serving you, and then you look up at a man with gold teeth, dreadlocks, five gold chains, and a shirt drenched in sweat from the heat of the dish room asking you, "You done with that chicken wing?" And before you can answer, he snatches the plate away from you and disappears back into the darkness. It was hilarious to see in action.

I had worked so many food service jobs where everyone did the bare minimum. No one at Golden Corral seemed to behave that way, and at the top of the food chain in this work ethic was Big Mixx. I asked Mixx one day why he was so hyperfocused on doing his job correctly.

He simply said, "'Cuz I ain't going back to jail. Man, these crackers ain't gonna have a reason to fire me. You gonna fire me, goddamn it, you gonna have to make up a reason, but it ain't gon' be 'cuz I ain't do the job. I ain't going back to jail."

One day, my probation officer told me he had to visit Golden Corral to verify my employment. I'd been dreading this day because I'd lied on the application and never told Golden Corral I'd been arrested. I hoped that I'd be able to charm them with my work ethic over the first few months, and that then when they found out the truth they'd be able to judge me on my body of work.

I came in that morning and confessed my secret to my manager, Mr. Galloway.

"Hey, man, a dude is going to come by here today who just needs to verify my work for some stuff," I said. I never used the word *probation* or *officer,* but Mr. Galloway knew what was up. "Oh, no problem," he said. "Let me know when he's here, and I'll show him around."

Later that afternoon, my probation officer came into the building. Khaki pants tighter than Adolfo's, a gun on his hip, a shimmering gold badge next to it, and one of those tight two-button polo shirts with an embroidered badge on his chest. Big Mixx had a radar for stuff like this. He peeped him right away. "Goddamn, that motherfucker got two badges on, one on his hip and one on his chest. You know somebody about to go to jail."

My probation officer walked around the restaurant, making sure that I was actually an integrated part of the team and not just there in a Golden Corral uniform pretending to have a job. A law enforcement officer walking around the store, not eating, got the undivided attention of the back of the house. Panic spread. They figured he was there to arrest somebody for a probation violation.

"Shit! I know it ain't me!" Big Mixx screamed over the hum of a loud industrial dishwasher. "I told y'all, man, I ain't going back to jail!" We all laughed at him, but the more my probation officer walked around, the more antsy the back of the house became.

All of a sudden Big Mixx was no longer interested in stalking the dining room for dirty dishes. Mike Lou quietly and contentedly re-cooked any food you brought out there without seeking feedback from the customers. God forbid they get spotted by this law enforcement officer if it turned out they were the one he was looking for.

When you are working in the front of the house, it's tough to keep up with the conversations happening in the back of the house because you only hear them in fragments, but every trip back to the dish room, the conversation was becoming more and more panicked.

"Well, I don't know who he is."

"Well, motherfucker, if he's not your police, and he ain't my police, then who the fuck police is he?"

"Well, go ask him."

"If he here, he here to arrest somebody. Did you piss dirty?"

"Hell no. My piss been clean for the last four or five months. I keep telling you, man, these crackers ain't gonna catch me slipping. I'm not fucking up no more."

My manager came out and talked to the probation officer, and they shook hands. Everybody in the restaurant looked on frantically. And then they saw my probation officer come over and shake my hand, and the cat was out the bag. Everyone there knew my secret. I was on probation.

After my probation officer left, my first trip was to Mr. Galloway's office for what I assumed was me being fired. But not only was Mr. Galloway understanding, he was excited. It turned out the state of Florida gave employment tax credit breaks to businesses that hired convicted felons. Mr. Galloway was starting to go through my paperwork so he could claim the tax credits that he would receive for the six months I'd been working there so far. As it turned out, this Golden Corral location took pride in giving second chances to people who had made mistakes, and the owner welcomed people like me with open arms. I couldn't have picked a better place to work.

I almost cried for joy in the office. I wasn't more than two steps out of Mr. Galloway's office before I was swamped by people in the back of the house wanting to know all the details of my probation.

"Man, I thought you was a schoolboy. What you did, murder? Dope? Ain't no way in hell your little ass on probation."

As I shared the details of my arrest, they in turn shared theirs. It was like an odd Felons Anonymous meeting. Everybody there who had done—or was currently on—some form of supervised release pulled me aside and told me their story, what they had been dealing with, and what their life was like. It was some of the most uplifting conversation I had ever had.

That day was the first day I ever truly felt that forgiveness was possible or even a real thing. It was the first day that gave me hope that my life wouldn't just be the sum of my mistakes. I was closer to and more respected by the back of the house after that. As far as they were concerned, I was one of them now. We are a country founded on religious principles of forgiveness and turning the other cheek, yet every piece of infrastructure is set up to remind you of and hold you accountable for your past mistakes. Your arrest record, your credit score, your driving history, your rental history—are all just measurements of morality that people use to establish a trust matrix about you.

From then on, I was protected and enveloped in the goodwill of everyone older than me at Golden Corral. Big Mixx and his cousin who also worked in the dish room would check on me from time to time. "Hey, young brother, you okay? How's everything going?" These constant check-ins were so important to me. Big Mixx was by far the most diligent. "Keep them grades good and that piss clean and leave them hoes alone. The pussy gone come. Achieve ya goals, you'll get the hoes." "Hey, little nigga, don't let these crackers catch you slipping," he'd say. "I'm telling you right now, that's what they're going to try to do. I'm not going back to jail." Big Mixx never talked in detail about his time in jail, and out of respect I never asked. But if Mr. Willie could share the horrors of war, then whatever was happening in prison must have truly been unspeakable.

Not only did I have friends and examples of how I should be carrying myself as a man, but there were checks and balances. If you weren't living right, if you didn't have your shit together, then you could get the hell on. It wasn't cool to get shit-faced drunk. It wasn't cool to do drugs. It wasn't cool to be all of these negative things. I learned accountability at Golden Corral.

I had a work family, and not only that, they were supportive of me pursuing comedy. Some Friday nights, RJ or Adolfo would sneak and cover my section while I raced up the street to the Ramada Inn to do a quick five-minute set at the comedy night they had up there. Shift leader Miss Darlene would even be kind enough to come to me first to see what days I would be in town before making the schedule for the rest of the staff. This saved me the trouble of trying to swap shifts with people so that I could still honor my road dates.

Things were chugging along pretty well for me. I had a girlfriend and I was slowly climbing the comedy ladder. That fall of 1999, Florida A&M allowed me to enroll again and resume pursuit of my journalism degree. I had a good rhythm. Then one day, one of the journalism students came up to me and said, "Hey, Roy, a guy died in a shootout yesterday with the Tallahassee police. He worked at Golden Corral, I wonder if you knew him." He took me to his desk and showed me the article he was writing. I saw the mugshot. It was Big Mixx. My heart dropped.

My initial feeling was sadness, but it was closely followed by fear. When you are on probation, you kind of live life looking back over your shoulder because you always feel like you're going to make an innocent mistake for which you will be prosecuted to the fullest extent of the law. *Am I next?* I wondered.

According to the police reports, Mixx had a domestic dispute with a woman and when officers had shown up to serve an arrest warrant for a probation violation. Mixx resisted and opened fire on the officers, and in the chaos he grabbed a child and used the child as a human shield as he continued to threaten the officers with the gun. Officers waited patiently until they had a clear shot, and then they killed Big Mixx and got the child to safety. I try not to act surprised when I hear about people doing things that you could not fathom them doing, but the truth is, do we ever know what anybody is truly capable of when they are cornered?

Big Mixx chose death over going back to prison. I don't know why he did that. But I have been around enough people who have gone to prison to know that it changes a man. The entire time I had thought that when this man proclaimed he was never going back to prison, it was a declaration of an intent, of living positively, a commitment to a better life. But it very well may have been him simply saying, "No matter what happens in my life, I will choose death before I go back into that place, and I'm willing to do any- and everything possible to facilitate that."

I'm still as shocked, saddened, and confused now as I was when I heard the news back then. Big Mixx was confirmation of what I had already suspected, that prison was a place I never wanted to go. I promised myself that I would never make a choice again that would make that a possibility for me. To have his positivity so rapidly devolve into desperation is still something I don't understand.

I worked at Golden Corral a little over two years. I never officially quit, I just kept calling off of work because I kept booking more road gigs. As I got into the back half of my senior year of college in 2001, Miss Darlene said to me, "You've been calling off a lot lately, and that means your comedy is going good. Instead of me putting you on the schedule, how about you call me when you are ready to come back to work."

"Yes, ma'am," I said humbly. "I will call you when I'm ready to work another shift." That was more than twenty-five years ago. I still haven't called them back, but I still have my Golden Corral name tag just in case.

CHAPTER 11

The Man from Philadelphia

Two things hit me immediately after I was arrested. One, I was lonely. Two, I was broke.

College is interesting in that you're almost never alone. You have a roommate, a bunch of classmates, and if you're fortunate, a group of friends. You eat lunch together, you play intramurals together, you pick up birthday strippers together. There's almost never a moment of solitude.

It's not until you're constantly sitting alone in your house that you realize how much of your entire social life was built around your being able to provide stolen goods to strangers.

I think, in a lot of ways, my choices were rooted in my desire to be liked. Whatever it took to fit in, I guess I was willing to do it. When I'd moved to Birmingham, I was never in the same school system more than two years until I got to high school. Now, in college, I'd finally been able to stop being the guy who nervously introduced himself to people, hoping they would like him. Everyone came to me and introduced themselves.

But once I got arrested and could no longer offer really good pizza at a really good price, I learned very quickly that a lot of people only like you based on what you are able to do for them.

That took some adjusting to.

Going from being a full-blown social butterfly to someone who ate all his meals alone, even when his roommates were in the house, was hard. Then I got hit with the ultimate death blow to my social life. Because I'd been working in the campus post office when I'd stolen the credit cards, I was in violation of the student code of conduct and Florida A&M suspended me for a semester.

In addition to not being able to attend any classes, I also could not show up to any social functions. This meant no tailgates, no basketball pep rallies, no fraternity parties, no nothing. They literally sent me a map of an area that was essentially a no-fly zone for me. And to top it all off, my trusty 1987 Dodge Aries K finally died. So now I didn't even have a car. I bought a mountain bike for seventy-five dollars from a pawnshop, and between that and riding the city bus for free with my student ID I found a way to get around town anyway.

I was incensed. I was embarrassed. I was depressed. I moved out into my own one-bedroom unit. It was lonely. I even missed the quasi–silent treatment me and my roommates were giving one another after my arrest. I figured the best thing for me to do was to stay in motion and make a little money. And I needed every penny. The money I was making from Golden Corral wasn't going to cut it, and there was no way in hell I was going to call my mom.

That year had been the toughest year my mother and I ever had experienced. She cried the first time I got arrested. She bawled the second time. She almost passed out when I got suspended from school. It was originally supposed to be an expulsion. I never told her that I had started doing comedy. I knew she wouldn't approve of it. So when I'd take the Greyhound up to Birmingham to perform in an open mic night once a month, I'd sleep at the bus station instead of my mother's house.

However, at this point, my mother was a college professor in Birmingham. One night, one of her students who worked at the bus station saw me sleeping on a bench. He snitched on me to my mom and it was on from there. She called me, furious.

"You need to be focused on that goddamn education. That college degree is your only chance of getting something decent out there in the job market. What the hell are you doing sleeping in a goddamn bus station?"

I didn't say much back to her other than just making it clear to her that I wasn't going to stop. Comedy was the only thing I loved. It was the only thing that mattered to me because on stage was the only time I truly felt happy. Because she made her disapproval of comedy clear to me, anytime my mother called and tried to make small talk, I immediately became evasive. Her intentions might have been genuine, but I was so on guard that I took any attempt at conversation as her trying to pry to see if I was still doing stand-up comedy. *The only thing I care about, you don't want me doing,* I thought. *So as far as I was concerned there was nothing for us to discuss.* Before my arrest my mother and I probably talked three or four times a week. But now in 1999, my mother and I talked once a month for a total of five minutes. And it would stay that way for most of the rest of 1999.

I'm still this way to this day. When someone is not supportive of something that I believe in and they do not respect my conviction about the issue, I shut down and share less with them. I was going to spend my time the way I wanted, happy and on the road doing stand-up comedy, and no one else was going to tell me what to do otherwise—not even her.

I needed to work because the other thing that happens almost overnight after getting arrested is you become broke. Like instantly. What little money you do have goes to lawyers to try and stay free. On top of probation the government imposed a $1,500 fine on me for my crimes. And at that age $1,500 might as well have been $40,000. Yeah, I was free, but freedom came at a cost.

Golden Corral was giving me only twenty hours a week and they weren't the best shifts to make tips. It was barely enough to pay rent and bills. If I needed anything else, it was going to have to come out of my own pocket, so I did whatever I could to make a little extra money. I would then take that money and use it to pay for bus tickets as I went from town to town building my career as a stand-up comedian.

I was finding knickknack jobs here and there, but it was never enough money. Then one day at work, like a dreadlocked gold-toothed guardian angel, Big Mixx said to me, "Shit, man, so long as you ain't doing cocaine or sticking your dick anywhere strange, these white folks will give you thirty or forty dollars for some of your blood." So off my gold-toothed Yoda's suggestion, I was able to settle in twice a week donating blood plasma.

The plasma centers in Tallahassee would give you seventy-five dollars per donation and you could donate up to twice a week. To keep you from donating more than the allotted two times, each center would stamp your hand with some ridiculously strong ultra-violet ink that wouldn't come off even in the shower. This way, if you went to another location, they would see the UV ink and know that you were already in the rotation somewhere else in town and deny you the right to donate.

Donating plasma more than twice a week is extremely un-healthy. I know this because one week I donated three times. After a few weeks, I learned that they always stamp your hand in the exact same place. So on the way to donate plasma for the first time that week, I went into my girlfriend's makeup bag and put some con-cealer on my hand to serve as a layer between my actual skin and the ultraviolet ink.

I gave plasma the way I normally did, and then afterward I washed my hands and the ultraviolet ink washed right off my skin. It was as if the first plasma donation of the week had never even happened. I then went across town the next day to another location and gave what was my second donation but in their system was my first. A few days later I went in for my third donation. After the third donation, I left the plasma center after the required thirty-minute wait time post donation. I was rolling in dough. The only thing I remember after I walked out the front door was waking up face down on a city bus, with a stranger slapping my face and asking me if I was okay.

A sweet white woman came up to me. "Young man, I think you fainted. Maybe you need to stay on this bus for a little while. Do you know where you are?"

As she reached out to help me back to my feet, another passenger slapped her hand out the way. "There ain't nothing wrong with that boy. That motherfucker is on drugs. I know drugs when I see 'em," he said, before turning to me. "You need to stay off them drugs, you are too young for drugs."

I staggered off the bus and don't really remember anything else from that day, but it was also the last time I gave plasma three times in one week.

As the summer of 1999 pushed on, my comedy gigs were taking me farther and farther away from Tallahassee, which was cutting into my hours at Golden Corral. I wasn't making enough on the road to make up the money I was losing at work, and I was having a hard time paying my rent.

I remembered reading either the *Thrifty Nickel* sales paper or one of the local newspapers and seeing advertisements for day labor and temp services.

Today, the term "day laborer" is generally used to describe someone who is working illegally without the proper paperwork. But back when I was in college, day laborer and temp were basically the same. The biggest difference is that most day laborer jobs were outdoors.

You would show up to these places early in the morning and wait in the lobby for an assignment, which could be anything from yard work to clerical work to construction work. It was literally the employment lottery. One day you could be working a football booster banquet and serving a plate of catfish to legendary Florida State football coach Bobby Bowden. The next day you could be standing off on the side of the road in an orange vest directing traffic around street-paving equipment. It wasn't always the best work, but it paid the bills.

I didn't make as much money doing day labor work, but it was far more flexible than Golden Corral. If one of my gigs canceled and I was stuck in Tallahassee on the weekend, I couldn't pick up a shift at Golden Corral unless somebody called off. It was far easier to just wake up on a Saturday morning and go down to the temp office and get a random job for the day. It was never fun work, but it was better than passing out on buses, and covered the hours that I was losing at Golden Corral because I was on the road more.

Thankfully, I was finally booking clubs in bigger cities that had comedy more than one day a week. This was the dream as a road comedian. My favorite place to do comedy during this time was Columbia, South Carolina. The Comedy House Theater was a six-night comedy room located in one of only three cities in the entire Southeast at the time that operated that many nights a week. Birmingham and Atlanta were the other two. But Columbia was better because if you were an emcee (the first comic on stage for the night) there, they booked you for two weeks straight. The booker didn't want the stress of booking a comedy club host every week.

You would perform Tuesday through Sunday, the club would cover your hotel on the Monday off day, and then you'd perform another Tuesday through Sunday. Performing in the same city multiple days also meant something important: I could get a day job at a temp service while I was there.

The Greyhound would get me into Columbia around 10 P.M. on a Monday night. Usually I could call and sweet-talk the front desk clerk at the hotel into letting me check in a day early to my room that the comedy club was paying for. If they did not, no problem, I would just sleep at the bus station. Tuesday morning I would wake up around 5:00 A.M., hop on mass transit, and head to the temp service offices to apply for work. The guy would ask you a few questions about your physical capabilities. "Do you own a pair of steel-toed boots? Do you have a problem with working outdoors?" "Does your back hurt?" "Can you lift shit?" Et cetera, et cetera.

You would then go sit in the waiting area and pray to God that your name was called for a work assignment that day. If you weren't called, then you were moved to the top of the list for the following day. You would essentially sit in the lobby and wait for random companies to call and say, "Hey, I need five people who can cut grass today," or "I need five people who can wait tables today." Because of this uncertainty, the lobbies of most day labor offices are depressing. Everybody has an expression on their face that looks like they are on their third trip to the Department of Motor Vehicles.

To say this place was bleak would be an understatement. It had its regulars, the guys coming in with a packed lunch. They had jeans with three days' worth of filth caked into the front thighs. I would later learn that dirty clothes were a badge of honor. If you showed up to a construction site on the first day and your clothes were already dirty, it was taken as a sign that you were willing to work. That type of tenacity could very well get you hired permanently on some of these jobs.

Some people were friends, but most people kept to themselves. It was clear no one wanted to be there. Then again, could you blame them? Showing up every day and going down to an office and playing job lottery isn't exactly what they told you to strive for at Career Day. But we all sat there quietly because for most of us, these moments in the office would be the last air conditioning we would feel for the next eight hours.

I enjoyed working day labor, mainly because of the camaraderie. Road comedy is basically professional isolation. Once the gig was done, you and the other comedians went your separate ways. I longed for connection in a way that I never had. I didn't have a big social network of friends in Tallahassee, and maybe some of what I craved from these men was mentorship and fatherhood—the kind I wasn't getting at Golden Corral anymore because I was always on the road. So I always looked forward to the conversations with the men that I did day labor with in Columbia.

I had some clerical skills, but because I was a big brawny young man clearing six feet and 250 pounds, no matter what, in South Carolina I always pulled an outdoor job. It was either some job on the freeway working way too close to the hot tar or some job out in the field for a couple of days helping to lay gravel to make a new parking lot. None of those days were easy, but they were very rewarding.

One of the tougher assignments, one of the hardest single days of physical labor I ever was a part of, was at the Quikrete factory. Underneath a large un-air-conditioned, unventilated aluminum shed, workers made and packaged this dry instant concrete mixture. The operation was pretty simple. It was an assembly line. At one end of the assembly line was a bag man. The job of the bag man was to take a flat, unfilled Quikrete bag and fit it onto a nozzle. The nozzle man sat in a chair high above the conveyor belt that ran underneath him and monitored the powder mixture descending from a maze of chutes and conveyor belts high above. He would pull the lever, and in an instant the bag that was on the nozzle would be filled to the brim with ten pounds of ready-to-ship Quikrete.

The nozzle man would quickly snatch this freshly filled bag off the nozzle, seal the bag, and let it fall to the conveyor belt about two feet below. As quickly as he removed the filled bag, the nozzle man would place a new empty bag on the nozzle and the process would repeat itself.

The filled bag of Quikrete would slowly creep down the conveyor belt until it reached the stacker. The stacker's job was to take each ten-pound bag and lay them evenly in a staggered fashion onto a forklift pallet that lay on the ground at the end of the belt. Once the first pallet was stacked to a certain height, the wrapper would take a large roll of cellophane and quickly envelop the stacks of Quikrete on the pallet like a spider wrapping its prey. A forklift driver would then swoop in to pick up the freshly wrapped forklift pallet and take the product out to a waiting flatbed eighteen-wheeler in the parking lot. Once that eighteen-wheeler was filled to the brim, it would pull off, a new eighteen-wheeler would pull in, and the process would repeat itself over and over all day in ninety-seven-degree heat and 100 percent humidity.

My first day on the Quikrete job, I came dressed for what I figured would be some relatively light physical work. As we gathered in the break room for the morning safety briefing, I could tell this was going to be a sweaty job, so I removed the Chicago Cubs hat that rested on my head, not wanting to ruin it with sweat. One of the older Black men came up to me and said, "You need to keep that hat on your head." I said, "Nah, I'm good," and he just grinned and kept moving. I wasn't qualified to drive a forklift, and I didn't have enough seniority to operate the nozzle, so I was a stacker. I stood at the end of the conveyor belt as a freshly stuffed ten-pound bag of Quikrete spat toward me. Tossing one ten-pound bag two feet onto a waiting forklift pallet is not that hard, but over the course of eight hours, lifting a ten-pound bag starts to feel like lifting a pickup truck.

Then came the heat. Not wearing a hat also meant I didn't have anything to catch sweat. Because the bags were not sealed airtight, every time you tossed a Quikrete bag onto the forklift pallet, a gentle plume of dry concrete powder would float up into the air. These plumes did not fall quickly back to the ground. They remained in the air like pollen. This dry concrete would mix with the sweat on my forehead and make a nice concrete sludge that would now ooze its way down my face. The more I wiped, the more I simply worked to mix the concrete with my sweat.

And it all got in my hair too. By the end of my shift I had little dry gray concrete naps in my head. I made fifty-two dollars that day and ended up spending fifteen of that on a fucking haircut before my show that night.

The upside to working day labor was that you could refuse to return to a worksite if you did not like the work conditions. And because you already had been employed the day before, you were at the top of the list for the first job assignments to come the next day. I finally had the seniority that I'd envied so many other people for having in the past.

"Quikrete need some folks today if you wanna go back over there," the hiring manager said. The look on my face gave him the answer he needed. Whatever he was about to say next about working in an aluminum shed he opted not to say.

He quickly pivoted to another assignment: "They building a church. They're getting ready to lay carpet. I think they need some people to touch up the subfloors if you want to do that." This sounded more my speed, so I accepted.

When I got there, what would one day be a megachurch sanctuary was just a naked gray concrete slab in a big-ass room about the size of a Walgreens with a ceiling height of a two-story mall. The room also was not air-conditioned, but there were a few fans positioned around, so there was some semblance of a breeze moving through the space.

The job that day was to scrape any blemishes off the concrete floor. Someone had put spackle on the ceiling to get the ceiling in order and that spackle had fallen down to the floor. Before they could lay the padding for the carpeting, we first needed to scrape up this spackle so that the surface could be even.

Sounded good to me. Anything was better than being the stacker inside of an aluminum hot pocket sleeve.

The work was grueling, but we got down there and started the process of scrape, scrape, scraping. If you've ever been to the dentist, the sound was like that of the sharp pick that the dentist uses to remove tartar during a teeth cleaning.

The supervisors onsite didn't really care whether you worked in pairs or not, but most people did find a partner so that they would have someone to talk to. One guy seemed to take a liking to me.

"What got you here?" he asked.

I deflected and said I was in town visiting family but still trying to make a little money. That was usually enough to get most guys off my scent. I did not like telling people I was in town to do stand-up comedy. It usually led to another round of questions that I did not feel like answering.

For the sake of being cordial, I asked him the same question, to which he replied, "I'm from Philadelphia. They had me locked up down here for five years. I just got out of prison three weeks ago. I'm staying at a halfway house and doing this during the day to get my money up before I go home to start my life again."

It was a lot to take in. I'd rather he had just said he was visiting family.

But the Man from Philadelphia was excited. He was truly excited about life and about all the possibilities that lay ahead of him. There was a woman back in Philadelphia he was trying to get to, but he didn't want her to see him like this, so he insisted upon working for a few months to get himself together first. He talked about how blessed he was and how he couldn't wait to taste McDonald's later this week. For him, that would be considered splurging.

The Man from Philadelphia approached our work with a degree of pride and happiness that I just did not have. I always thought the unwritten agreement with manual labor was that you would rather be doing something else: that you would rather be making more money, but these were the cards that life had dealt you. The ethics of manual labor and of a construction site were much, much different from that of a restaurant or any other job I'd had.

Nobody really spoke to one another until it was break time.

There wasn't a lot of chitchat, and happiness was not the prevalent emotion, exhaustion was. I appreciated the conversation with the Man from Philadelphia. It made the time go by pretty fast. And I didn't even notice the raw blisters that had formed on the inside of my thumb from holding the scraper too tightly.

The day dragged on and he again asked me the same question, "What got you here?" And again I said, "I'm visiting family and I want to make some extra money." That lie bounced off of him like a rock off a tank.

"Man, who the fuck hate they family so much, they drive all the way to South Carolina to visit them, just to not be around them?" he said. "Look around you. Ain't nobody here on purpose. Everybody that's here right now, at this church, is here for a purpose. Ain't nobody here *on* purpose. They're here because they lack purpose."

I stopped scraping for a moment and I looked around for the first time at everyone working in the church. There were about thirty or forty of us. We were all pretty disheveled. Everybody was down on their luck. We represented every race, every height, every build, but we all had the same drab facial expression. No one in this building had purpose. I'm pretty sure the only person who had some degree of purpose was the man who was paying everyone to build them a church.

Then the Man from Philadelphia asked, "What do you notice about everyone in this room?"

"They're all working?" I replied.

"*No!*" he snapped back at me. "No. Just about everybody in this room at least forty or damn near. You barely twenty-three. So I'm going to ask you again. What are *you* doing *here*?"

That was the first time the idea of a life with purpose landed with me. He was telling me I still had a chance.

I looked at the huge crucifix that hung on the back wall of the church and just stared at it for a while. Maybe it was God sending me a message through this man. If he was, I for sure got it.

I looked back down at Philly and I said, "I understand what you're saying now." He said, "Do you?" And I said, "Yeah, I understand you, bro."

He said, "Good. So you see what I see. They're old, you're young! If I were you, I would be working extra hard."

"Excuse me?" I said.

"You are the youngest person on this worksite by at least ten, maybe fifteen years," he said excitedly. "If there's anybody who has a chance of getting a permanent hire on this worksite, it's *you*."

I was confused, but the more he talked, the more I put it all together.

"Look, man," he continued, even more excited. "You have so much potential here, young brother. The world is yours. This is how it works here. You come here for a week and you just do the job, and they have to pay you the regular salary that you negotiated at the temp office. But see, what they are actually doing is using the temp service as a way to find viable long-term employees. This ain't a job, man, it's an audition. The more they use the same people, sooner or later, they got to give you a bump. See, right now we're making seven dollars an hour, but I guarantee if you come here and work hard, after two weeks, they have to give you a bump to seven fifteen. After a month, seven and a quarter. If they bring you on permanent, that's seven fifty. Hell, that might even be eight dollars. That's good money right there."

Philly sat there on his knees next to me, scraping away with a huge smile on his face as he fantasized about making $7.50 an hour.

I was pretty much mortified at that point. I had thought this man saw potential in me to not live this life. But what he saw in me was the fact that, because I'd entered this life so early, I had a chance to be making far more money than him by the time I got to his age.

It basically felt like he was saying to me, "You threw your life away at an early enough age that you could actually make some real money in this alternate universe that you've now been banished to."

The job that I'd considered a quick way to grab cash while in town pursuing something else, he saw as a permanent means to an end. For many people it is, and that's fine, but I wanted something different for myself.

I really looked Philly in the eyes this time, and those eyes were dead. Up until my arrest, I had had it in my head that I was going to be the next Stuart Scott. I didn't know what my fate would be now, considering that ESPN would probably never hire a convicted felon. All I knew was that I enjoyed doing comedy, but if there was going to be any chance of me ever doing anything else in life, I was going to need that college degree. It wouldn't completely offset a felony conviction on a job application, but it would be a good start.

The conversation with the Man from Philadelphia horrified me, and it got me the fuck together. Talking to him was like talking to someone who had been so defeated by the system, who had lost so much hope for themselves, that all they wanted was their freedom and a decent job. For sure those are two amazing things to have, but I still had things I wanted to do with myself. I wasn't yet ready to become the really good employee at a job I did not love.

I kept working at the church for the next two weeks that I was in Columbia, but I didn't talk to the Man from Philadelphia that much after that day. He was turned off of me a few days later because he felt I "took too many water breaks" and wasn't working hard enough.

That was a long bus ride back to Florida that summer. But if I didn't know anything else, I knew I wanted the best possible opportunity to build a decent life for myself, and I knew that would come only with a college degree. When I got back to Tallahassee from that trip, I called my mother.

"Hey, I would like to offer a deal," I said. "If I can get back in school this fall and I make the dean's list, you and I never again discuss me doing stand-up comedy. Stand-up comedy is important to me, and getting an education is important to you. I will pursue my education while doing stand-up comedy, and so long as my grades are strong, you have to let me do that without criticism."

There was a long stretch of silence on the phone, so long it almost felt like the call had dropped. Then my mother's voice casually broke the silence.

"That's fine by me."

I replied, "Good, now, if I'm going to have any chance of getting back into college, some people are going to have to write some letters of recommendation for me. Let's discuss who I should get to write them."

I don't know if I ever would have seen and realized the value of an education, if not for the Man from Philadelphia. The college degree in broadcast journalism that I eventually got from Florida A&M University has paid me dividends one-hundred-fold.

My suspension was lifted and I was back in school that fall. I was a man of my word and I made the dean's list that semester. The one thing I did not tell my mother, though, was that I condensed all of my classes to Tuesday through Thursday so that I could have Friday and Monday to ride the Greyhound anywhere I wanted.

My grades were so good that by the end of 1999, our relationship started to thaw. She actually started asking me questions about stand-up comedy. She had no choice. There were no bad grades to berate me about. There were no professors to call. For the first time since maybe tenth grade, my mother stopped worrying about my future. Because she no longer needed to worry about who I was becoming as a student, she started to explore who I'd become as a person. That winter we began to heal.

For my birthday that year we talked for about an hour. It was the first time we had talked for more than ten or fifteen minutes in a year. It was good to have my teammate back again. I told her some pretty funny stories about things that I had seen on the Greyhound bus. From fistfights to drug use to masturbation to people shitting with the door open because the lock was broken, It was all pretty hilarious to me, but it horrified her enough to put down a payment on a car. For Christmas of 1999 my mother gifted me a 2000 Ford Focus.

"All I did was make the down payment, you gotta keep up the car note."

To this day I don't know what made my mother buy that car, but it is the second single greatest thing she ever did for me in my life, the first being her decision to move us to Birmingham so I could have a father.

She gave me the car on one condition. That I call her every Monday to let her know I got back to Tallahassee safely. I kept my word and a conversation that was at first just me sharing that I was alive eventually evolved into me telling her how the gig went, to how my week went, to how my life was going. It remains a weekly conversation we have to this day.

I was back in school and I had wheels and for the first time in my life I had real purpose—and I owe a lot of that to a man from Philadelphia.

CHAPTER 12

Cry Baby

My Uncle Derix was the first man I ever saw cry. And when I say cry, I don't mean a single tear running down your cheek because your team won the game. When I say cry, I mean uncontrollable weeping and convulsing, snot coming out of your nose. Sobbing so intense that you literally do not recognize this person you thought you knew well because they're so emotionally incapacitated.

Uncle Derix's crying was wild to witness in person. He remains the manliest man I've ever known. A tall man towering around six foot four with broad shoulders that carried the burdens of PTSD from years of military service, Derix rough-and-tumbled with the slickest of Clarksdale, Mississippi, street hustlers before settling down and having two children. He has the physical build of a backup NFL quarterback, and the mobility of one who has about three games left in his career, but make no doubt about it, he's strong enough to strangle an ox with his bare hands.

All of that went out the window the day his wife, my Aunt Mary, was killed by a drunk driver. It really caught the family off guard. Aunt Mary was very kind and always nurturing. Quiet and soft-spoken, she was the perfect counter to Derix's loud and boisterous nature. She was his world. She was his balance.

Aunt Mary's funeral was also the first funeral I went to. I was in second grade at the time, and I think as a child, you have to first observe people grieving before you know how to approach it. My uncle went up to his wife's casket with his two children and he just broke down. I'd never seen anything like it. I understood he was sad, but I'd never watched grief and frustration wash over someone that way. To this day I've never talked to my uncle about my aunt's death. I just don't feel like it's my place.

The second—and most memorable—time I ever saw a man cry was when I was around the eighth or ninth grade. My dad had been splitting time between our home and the home of Valerie, the mother of my two younger brothers. Much like Aunt Mary, Valerie died unexpectedly. It was devastating to my father. It broke him.

When I was around my dad, I always felt like I was the child by the other woman and my two younger brothers and their mom were his real family. He was out with Valerie so much in public, there are still people in Birmingham who think that she was my mother. Attending this funeral confirmed for me that Valerie was the woman he loved. It was all a very weird thing for me to experience in the moment, but ultimately I just went to the funeral to be there for my little brothers.

I rode with my father and my two younger brothers in the limo in the funeral procession, but once we were in the church, I drew the line at sitting in the front row. Valerie wasn't my mom, so I nestled in on the back side of the church, maybe ten or twelve pews back, and I just observed. Everyone passed this woman's casket to pay their respects. When it was my father's turn, he broke down. One of the most hardened, shit-talking men I've ever known was reduced to a pile of rubble in front of the casket of the woman whom I'm sure he would've rather have spent the rest of his life with.

Over the years I've had glimpses of my two parents where I could see what attracted them to each other. But here in this moment, at this funeral, was the first real time I saw my father in love.

My dad sobbed over that casket. I didn't even know he had those types of emotions in him or that he was even capable of that level of love. I watched him as he held my two younger brothers tight as if to say, "I got you. We're going to get through this." I sat in the back of this woman's funeral, jealous of the version of my father she'd gotten to experience. Neither my father nor Uncle Derix was the same after those funerals.

I'll give them both credit. They were both fucked up pretty good by those deaths, but the one thing both of them did, sooner or later, was get back to living. It took my uncle a little longer than it did my dad, but to be fair, my dad was way older than my uncle and had seen way more shit that one would argue is even worse than a war.

In 2002, it was my turn to cry.

I'd graduated college a year earlier and had moved back in with my mom in Birmingham. I was still sleeping on the same twin bed from my childhood when my phone rang one morning.

"Hey, Roy, it's Ben Hill, executive producer of *It's Showtime at the Apollo*."

"Yes, sir, Mr. Hill," I said, springing to my feet.

"How would you like to appear on this season of *It's Showtime at the Apollo*?"

I don't even think I said words after that, I think I only made sounds of joy.

"We are taping the show in a week. I will email you all the details," he added. "Please bring multiple outfits, in case you advance to the next episode of the show. We will not provide hotel or airfare, but there will be a few snacks in the green room."

"Not a problem! Yes, sir," I said.

The entire call took less than ninety seconds. After I hung up, I sat and gave myself a fist bump. I looked at myself in the mirror in the bathroom, screaming with excitement. Finally, it was my fucking turn. Finally, it was my fucking time.

It was one of those calls where you are so excited that other people in the house come stand around you because they're anxious to hear what good news you've just received. My mom stuck her head in the door of my bedroom and I simply gave her a thumbs-up. She smiled and went about her day.

It's Showtime at the Apollo was the premier televised showcase for Black talent in the '90s. If you successfully navigated Amateur Night there, it could open a lot of doors for you with regard to getting talent management, bookings, and more. The show's popularity and relevance were starting to wane in the 2000s as more places for new Black talent to pop up started to emerge across cable television. But if nothing else, in 2002 the show was the perfect place to show off your skills and get booked on a more popular show.

Amateurs who had never been on television before would go on stage and perform for two to three minutes and the crowd would either cheer or boo you. If you got booed, then a person called the Sandman would dance his way up to you and comically escort you off the stage. His routines were very funny, and when he mocked you, it was kind of a cherry on top for the audience—a reward for doing such a great job rejecting a stranger's talents.

Luckily, I wasn't going to be a part of the traditional Amateur Night portion of the show. I would be part of a new showcase called Comedy TKO. Producers felt that stand-up comedy couldn't be fairly judged as part of an Amateur Night's cavalcade of talents. There's no punch line that's going to beat someone nailing a Whitney Houston high note. And there's no way you're going to write a joke that is more adorable than a young child performing well above their age.

The premise of Comedy TKO was simple. Two comedians went

head-to-head, each performing for three minutes. The audience decided on a winner, and that person advanced to the next episode, until there was a grand champion at the end of the season.

I wasn't even down off my high before my phone rang again. It was my comedian friend Henry.

Before I could say hello, Henry was screaming into the phone, "Yeah, nigga. Yeah, nigga. If I got the call I know you got the call! Did you get the call?"

I said, "Yeah, motherfucker, I got the call!"

Henry's excitement pierced my ear canal like a well-aimed needle. "You damn right we goin' to New York. This is it, man, we are about to be stars! I just called my baby mama and cussed her out and told her I don't need to live with her anymore because I'm about to be a fucking star. I put the house key on the counter!"

Henry and I were around the same age—twenty-three, maybe twenty-four years old—and had been doing comedy about the same amount of time. He was the closest thing I had in the industry to a peer. But because we were road comedians, we did not see each other often. Performing in the South leaves you far more isolated than the comedians who hang with one another every night in the big cities. We had a lot of the same gripes about the industry, including how so much of ascending in the world of Black comedy involved political games that he and I refused to play. This was a chance to skip a level and, as I put it, land myself a role in an Ice Cube movie.

"See, man, the same thing that happened to Chris Tucker is going to happen to us. We will kill it on this show, Ice Cube will see us, put us in a movie, and then we will be stars." I had it all figured out.

"Hey, man, we should split a hotel room," I said.

"Whatever you find is fine by me."

I did an internet search and found a pretty affordable hotel close to New York, the Knights Inn, in Elizabeth, New Jersey. The pictures were decent, but I didn't really care about the aesthetic. They had me at the price: thirty-five dollars a night. Seventeen dollars a night felt like the perfect split for two young men in their early twenties living with people that they were anxious to get away from.

Henry and I decided we'd go to New York City two or three days before the show with the hopes of getting a little bit of stage time in the New York City area to see how our jokes would translate to an East Coast audience. I arrived at the hotel around 9:00 or 10:00 P.M., an hour or two before Henry. As I pulled into the horseshoe-shaped, one-way-in, one-way-out entrance, it dawned on me that I'd made one major miscalculation. These were the days before people left accurate travel reviews. I had no idea the hotel I'd picked was in a neighborhood that was a den for open-air drug dealing and prostitution.

Sex workers strutted up and down the street in brightly colored platform heels. From underneath their trench coats you could catch an occasional peek of a flashy skirt that was far too short for the January wind chill in the tristate area. Interspersed between these women were a lot of rough-looking guys. Some might have been pimps, but the rest were for sure drug dealers. For me it was easy to tell the difference.

Drug dealers have a higher situational awareness than the average person walking down the sidewalk. The constant swiveling of their heads from left to right indicates that they're looking out for the police or a rival crew. Either way, they are in a perpetual state of fight or flight. The few pimps that I have seen in my travels were all pretty calm, relaxed even.

I had no idea how to relay to Henry that I had probably picked the worst possible hotel for us to stay at. And we had to stay there because I'd made a nonrefundable reservation. I had just enough money on me to eat once a day. I'd used the rest of my cash to pay all of the tolls and bridge fees that come with traveling pretty much anywhere north of Washington, D.C.

The "front desk" of the hotel was simply a window with a slot underneath the bulletproof glass for you to slide your credit card and ID through. And that slot wasn't even wide enough for you to slide both of them through at the same time. A couple of the women came from the curb and stood a little closer to me, as though they were trying to get out of the wind and stay warm. But I knew they were eavesdropping and checking me out to figure out what my deal was.

"You need some company tonight, young man?" a woman said to me.

"No, ma'am," I said.

"Well, aren't you polite," she said while clocking my license plate. "We need more men like you out here, Mr. Alabama Man."

I got my keys and hustled to my room in my New Jersey crack lodge. Through one of the walls I could hear women having sex, and through the other I could hear some weird couple doing drugs together and inevitably getting into an argument. It was a Dolby Digital surround sound of bad ideas, poor life choices, and terrible noises.

Henry pulled in not too long after me. I came outside and tried to explain what the situation was, and he laughed it off. "Man, nigga, I'm from Memphis. I know about pimps and hoes, I'm right at home."

The room was exactly where you'd think a prostitute would take a customer she only planned to fuck for an hour. The sheets were so filthy, we slept on top of them fully clothed. The bed was a little too small for us to sleep comfortably next to one another, so we took turns. One person would take the bed, and the other person would sit in the chair next to the bed and extend their legs onto the open side of the mattress. It felt like falling asleep in one of those uncomfortable chairs that is next to a hospital bed.

The conditions were terrible, but we were on cloud nine. We spent most of the day at the hotel taking turns going outside to work on our jokes away from each other. We needed to perfect our sets. Oddly, though, when you're outside in a drug and sex market, and you aren't buying drugs or sex, you tend to make the people who are selling drugs and sex a little nervous. On top of that, Henry and I both had cars with out-of-state plates. And we did not look like what they would consider to be a gay couple. The locals could not figure us out. So no matter whether we went outside to take a break from working on our comedy set or to walk to the outdoor vending machines or to hop in our car on a quick food run, we were being watched. We made everyone uneasy.

The second afternoon in the parking lot, the inevitable happened. One of the women made her way over to me. A cigarette never left her lips the entire time she talked to me. She had on a tight red miniskirt that stopped exactly where her panties began—or at least where her panties were supposed to have begun. I'm not completely sure that she was wearing any, and I didn't want to stare long enough to obtain information.

"Is y'all the police?" the Woman in Red asked.

I said, "No, ma'am. And we ain't no snitches either. We ain't got no problem with whatever y'all doing."

As we spoke, I noticed some of the men on the street repositioning themselves so that they would be able to maintain an eye line on us as we talked.

"Well, if you ain't the fucking police, then who are you? I know y'all ain't on vacation because people on vacation don't take separate cars. Also people on vacation don't stay around here." I stood in awe of her detective work, but I believe that my silence only drove her to dig deeper. "Look, you don't have to tell me what you're doing or why you're around here. I was just curious, baby, it's a free country. It's just weird to me, you ain't bought no dope and you ain't bought no pussy, and that's just odd to me considering where you are right now."

I was unfamiliar with the customs in New Jersey. I didn't know that apparently buying a small piece of crack rock was the hospitable thing to do when visiting someone's hotel. Maybe it is equivalent to taking your shoes off when you enter somebody's home in the South.

The Woman in Red seemed genuine enough, so I decided to tell her the truth.

I explained to her who I was and what my friend and I were doing. "I'm a comedian. Me and my boy getting ready to perform at the Apollo Theater. We just coming outside, going over our jokes 'n' shit, so we ain't in there on top of each other." I told her this and her eyes lit up.

"Oh baby, when you get up on *that* stage? Oh baby, you got to do yo' thing at the Apollo. They rough up there. You need to make sure when you get onstage at the Apollo that you bring it."

She called over another man. He was big and rugged and wearing a black leather bomber jacket that had been rendered a dingy gray by years of wear and exposure to New Jersey winters. The cold January air tore into the dry skin on his hands, which seemed to be unaffected by the wind chill. Those hands had never seen lotion or the inside of a pocket for warmth. My best guess is the calluses that had formed on his hands also served as built-in gloves. It was hard to tell if he was a drug dealer or a pimp, or security for both of the aforementioned, but Bomber Jacket was for sure someone of rank and relevance.

He shuffled over to size me up.

"Tell him what you just told me," the Woman in Red said.

I looked at the man and the bomber jacket and again repeated why I was in town.

"See!" the Woman in Red said to Bomber Jacket. "Told you them lil niggas ain't up to nothing. He a schoolboy."

Bomber Jacket looked me up and down.

"From Alabama, huh?"

"Yes, sir," I replied. "We just up here trying to shake some shit."

"I got people down south."

"We all do, that's where the white folks dropped us off," I said jokingly. He didn't crack a smile. It was like his soul was impervious to humor.

"Where in Alabama?"

The more Bomber Jacket talked, the more the conversation started to take on the tone of an interrogation. *Am I being too honest?* I wondered. *Should I start lying?* I weighed these questions for about half a second before answering, "Birmingham."

Bomber Jacket paused for a minute as if he was deciding on the truthfulness of the answer.

"Aiight, you can stay here. You a honest motherfucker. I respect that. I got people, we ran your license plate the other day. I already knew the answer to them questions."

I don't know if he was telling the truth, but I was happy I hadn't lied. A man who doesn't use his own jacket pockets is a different level of crazy. He didn't shake my hand or dap me up or anything, he simply gave me a nod of approval as if to say Henry and I were officially cleared to remain on the premises. And in return, everyone outside working on the sidewalk could finally have peace of mind that we were not there to fuck up their money. The whole conversation with Bomber Jacket felt like a nightclub bouncer was deciding whether you met the dress code for his establishment. That was good enough for me. The rest of the way, the vibes were good at the Knights Inn even if the locals were a little sketchy.

That night, after doing a couple of sets around town and watching other comedians perform, I pulled up back at the hotel. I walked over to the vending machine near the front desk to get myself a soda. The Woman in Red sauntered over. "Them jokes do good tonight?"

"Yes, ma'am," I replied.

"Well, I think you're going to do good. If you come this far to chase this shit, you're already halfway home. That Apollo Theater is huge. I saw Lauryn Hill there, and one time I saw Mary J. Blige. They had some voices on them."

The more the woman talked, the more it felt like she was talking to herself and reminiscing. She had that look we all have when we're working a job that we wish we didn't have to work. That same lost look, that longing for something more. We chatted for two or three minutes more, just about the general state of comedy and entertainment. She was a huge Chris Tucker fan and loved him in the movie *Friday*.

"Who knows?" the Woman in Red asked as we said good night. "Maybe one day I will see you in one of those movies. Maybe you will be up there with Mike Epps."

That night I barely slept as I restlessly went over my set as best I could.

■ ■ ■

The next morning, it was game day. Henry and I hopped into my Ford Focus, and off to the Apollo Theater we went. The thing they don't tell you about performing at the Apollo Theater is how communal an experience it is. It's a small theater and they tape multiple episodes of the talent show on the same day, so there could easily be anywhere from fifteen to twenty different variety acts, all sharing an open green room space about the size of the average convenience store.

I don't remember his name, but there was a guy there in his sixties and his talent was roller-skating to Lou Rawls's music. That's it. Nothing else. Just a man on stage doing a slow-dance performance on roller skates. I found it to be such a hilariously random talent. You're not going to get invited onto *The Tonight Show* as the roller-skating dancing Black guy. But that was the beauty of *It's Showtime at the Apollo*. If you were Black and you had a gift, it did not matter what your gift was. This was the place to come and show it to the world. The show was a celebration of Blackness and Black talent, and not since that day have I felt more warmth in a space or more of a sense that my gift was relevant and worth sharing with the world.

That love and warmth stopped when you left the green room. The moment you went upstairs to go onstage and showcase your talents for all of Harlem, you were going to get punched in the fucking face by thousands of belligerent people who demanded the pinnacle of entertainment.

There are a few other things they don't tell anyone about *Showtime at the Apollo* that, in my opinion, have a direct effect on your performance.

First, in those days, the tickets to the TV tapings were free because they wanted to ensure a packed crowd.

Second, they sold alcoholic beverages and they were cheap. You could get vodka or whiskey or white wine all for about three dollars apiece.

Third, the Apollo Theater appears big on camera, but it's actually a very shallow room. And while most traditional theater shows leave the audience in darkness, the audience is essentially a character in *Showtime at the Apollo* so they have to be lit. Because they are so close, you can see every single face and every single microaggression when you are up there.

Last, they don't tell you that when's it's time to record the episode, they shoot the show in a nonlinear order and also use the same audience to shoot multiple episodes. Each episode of *Showtime at the Apollo* featured a two-song performance by popular Black artists at the time. So if they were shooting two episodes with one crowd, there would first be four earth-shattering performances by Black music legends.

A crowd full of Black people who hadn't paid to get in, and who'd been drinking three-dollar vodka, all got a free DMX concert. Then, after DMX, out walked Mary J Blige to do her two songs, or maybe it was Nelly, or The Lox. It didn't matter. That room was shaking.

After they taped a block of music acts, they did two groups of Amateur Night contestants, which meant about ten performances of two minutes each. As the night dragged on, Henry and I talked to each other less and less as we got into our respective zones. We got to the venue around 6:00 P.M., but it was probably closer to 10 P.M. when it was time for Comedy TKO to finally happen.

Finally, it was my turn. Impatience has a way of pushing stage fright out of your system when you have been waiting all night to change your life. I was facing off against a comedian from Miami, Dexter Angry. I didn't know Dexter or anything about his style of comedy. This was a major disadvantage in a competition because I could not predict what type of material he was going to perform. If I knew the caliber of comedian he was, then I could better decide whether to burn my best material now or to save my better jokes for a later round, assuming that I could defeat him with some of my weaker material.

Dexter Angry went out first and did great. There were no soft spots in his set. The jokes all connected. The host Rudy Rush immediately brought me out next. I don't remember all the jokes I did that night, but I do remember my biggest issue was that my material was, as I like to call it, "too long to the punch line." I didn't get the quick chuckles that you need when you're asking an audience to wait for a hard punch line thirty to forty-five seconds later. When you have only three minutes, thirty to forty-five seconds with no laughs is a fucking eternity. In my case it was a death sentence.

By the time I got to my first punch line, it barely connected. Around two minutes in, I started hearing boos. There weren't a lot, but it was enough to rattle me. I knew if I did one more joke I was going to get fully booed, so rather than do my final joke, I told the audience good night and walked off the stage forty-five seconds early.

As I stepped offstage, the show's producer Ben Hill was feverishly motioning for me to stay out there. I knew what the producers wanted—they wanted the sensationalism of the Sandman coming out to dance me off the stage. But it was the ultimate in humiliation as a performer, and there was no fucking way I was turning around and going back out there to finish my act.

At this point, it was time for me and Dexter Angry to be brought back out onstage where the audience could vote on who they liked more. Rudy Rush stood nearby while his cohost Kiki Shepard came out and stood next to us like a gorgeous ebony-skinned Vanna White.

"Okay, it's your time to vote," Rudy Rush said. "Show your love for Dexter Angry." A high-decibel wave of exultation enveloped the stage. The crowd cheered and screamed. "Okay, audience, now show your love for Roy Wood Jr." That same love was immediately vacuumed out of the room and replaced with boos. They booed and they booed hard. It seemed like forever. If you ask me, it was worse than what would have happened during my performance. At least if I'd gotten booed during my performance, the Sandman would have come out and gotten me off the stage. But now I couldn't go anywhere. I just had to stand there and take it. You can't escape your fate.

Dexter was announced as the winner, and I shook his hand and showed him respect. Then I descended back into the Green Room of Love. Most performers, no matter how you do, return to the green room to a resounding round of applause from other performers waiting to go on stage. The smatterings of applause felt good, but I was ready to go home. And I couldn't. I was driving Henry and he still hadn't performed.

I went back upstairs and watched the other rounds of Comedy TKO. There was this woman from Baltimore, Queen Aishah, who absolutely rocked that theater. You could feel the building seismically shifting from the power of her voice. I thought the first tier of the balcony was going to collapse after her punch lines. Her performance that night remains one of the single most raucous performances of stand-up comedy that I have ever witnessed.

Finally, it was Henry's turn. He went on stage and he got it worse than I did. After a joke or two, the audience just decided they did not like him. The Black experience is communal, familial almost, so rejection feels like being booed by your aunt, your uncle, and your cousin. If you're not careful, it can make you very angry. While I had decided to simply leave the stage, with the few seconds Henry had before the Sandman came out, he cursed out the audience.

It absolutely was not the right thing to do, but it was also absolutely beautiful.

"Y'all didn't even give a nigga a chance. If you ain't gon' even listen to the whole joke, then what the fuck is the point? All of you motherfuckers can kiss my motherfucking ass. Fuck you. Thank you very much. My name is Henry."

He then flung his microphone like a Frisbee what must have been at least ten to fifteen rows deep in the crowd. As he turned to walk off stage the microphone came hurtling back, flipping end over end like a battle-ax soaring through the air in a medieval battle. It didn't come close to hitting Henry, but just the idea that someone had the idea to throw the microphone right back, rather than lie down and collect their lawsuit money, shows you the essence of an Apollo crowd that has been drinking cheap wine and vodka for the last three hours.

It's still one of the funniest things I've ever witnessed at a live event.

Henry quickly found me in the back of the room and was anxious to leave. I wanted to stay and at least watch the other comedians, but considering I had gotten booed and Henry had basically cursed in church, we both had an odd aura around us. And the

microphone throw had made Henry persona non grata. The entertainment industry is weird in that one minute you can be onstage
with a chance to change your life (and be in an Ice Cube movie),
and in under thirty minutes, you're back outside in the freezing
cold that is Harlem in January, looking for your car.

We hopped into the Ford Focus and began the forty-five-minute
drive back to Elizabeth, New Jersey. In the car there was only
silence. Then, after about twenty minutes, a tear or two crept down
Henry's cheek. It wasn't a sob, it was a slow weep. I started crying
too.

This was supposed to be our moment, this was supposed to be
our time. We might never get this close to success ever again.

I don't even think we looked at each other. We were just two
men alone together, feeling our emotions. When we got back to the
Knights Inn, Henry spoke for the first time.

"Man, now I gotta call this girl and see if she'll give me my house
key back," he said with a big sigh.

We sat in the car and laughed for about five minutes straight at
the realization that we were right back to our regular lives. This life-
changing moment didn't change our lives and we were again forced
to face the reality of our diminutive existence. Henry continued,
"Hey man, I'm going to drive back right now. If I'm going to be
awake sitting in a chair and just being pissed off, it might as well
be the front seat of my car."

Henry ran in the room and grabbed his things, and then he
drove off. I remained in my car. When a door closes on you, it's hard
to realize that there are many other doors and that the door you're
knocking on might not even be a relevant door by the time someone opens it for you. But it doesn't feel like that in the moment. It
feels like everything is over. It feels like everything you've worked
for, every opportunity, has been shut down.

I cried in frustration. I had made what I'd considered to be some
major sacrifices to try and make this career work for myself.

The silence was broken by a gentle tap on the window. It was the Woman in Red. Off my face alone, I guess she could tell it hadn't gone as planned.

"Somebody had a bad night?" she asked.

As I looked up at her to formulate a response, I noticed she had a bruise on her neck. I jokingly replied, "Shit, you tell me."

"If you were as funny then as you are right now, you wouldn't be sitting in this car crying now, would you?" she said. I smiled. "Don't worry about my neck, some of these motherfuckas like to choke you. It pays extra."

She paused.

"Shit be like this sometimes, baby. Take your time to feel the pain, and when you're ready, get back to work. No matter what, you have to go back to work."

She leaned down to get a glimpse of herself in my side-view mirror to make sure she still looked presentable for potential customers. After she concluded her review, she stared at herself for an extra second or two longer.

"Yep, feel the pain, then get back to work."

We shared a couple seconds of silence as we both assessed our wounds, hers visible, mine internal. Bomber Jacket yelled out from across the parking lot.

"How'd Alabama do?"

"He got booed," I said.

"He'll be aiight. I got shot three times, I'm still here."

He delivered this fact with the simplicity of life all wrapped into it. I couldn't help but wonder if the man had gotten shot on three different occasions or if he'd gotten shot three times in a single shooting. As curious as I was for more details, it didn't seem like the time or place to seek clarification.

That night at the Apollo Theater was the first major loss in my career. I felt like I'd had an opportunity to enter a new level, to enter a new dimension of my career, and I'd failed. And it had taken so long to get this opportunity, there was no telling when the next one was going to come, so I was scared. But over the years I've learned, if you need to cry, cry, but sooner or later, you've got to get back to work.

Son, I saw you fall off your bike one day when you were seven. We were at your grandmother's house, and I was sitting in the front driveway with a good vantage point. You were about three or four houses down from me, and you took a nasty spill over the front of the handlebars and skinned up your knee pretty good.

I was hesitant to rush to your assistance because I wanted to see how good you were at soothing yourself in these instances. And I watched you. You felt the pain. You looked up at me, but you didn't call out this time. It was almost as if you didn't want me to come. You got up and dusted yourself off. You assessed your injuries. You assessed the state of your bike. You were crying, but you were composed, and you simply walked back to the house, where I tended to your wounds.

I don't know what the requisite amount of time is to feel pain and hurt before returning to oneself. I think that length of time will forever remain relative. But in that moment, I saw some of me in you—the ability to feel failure but also feel the need to get up and get back to it.

I am not sure if I should be proud of that or afraid, but for now, I'm proud.

CHAPTER 13

A Man of His Word

S on, so long as a man has his word, he's never truly bankrupt.

My independent upbringing has rarely left me in a position where I ever needed a favor. Casual favors, sure. I've scored a ride home from work or convinced a friend to help me move or asked a classmate to let me borrow a textbook I'd forgotten to order, but a *real* favor? No. I've always believed that I needed to solve my problems myself. Ask to borrow money? Forget about it. I'd rather die. That ethos prevented me from asking my mother for money in school, and it's what got me put on probation in the first place. But there was one time when there was no getting around it—I needed someone's help and their word meant everything. Turns out, it was one of the most important conversations of my early career.

This story starts back when I was still in college, where I was a sports and entertainment reporter for my college paper, *The Famuan*. No matter what I pitched, my academic adviser, Dr. Valerie White, and my editor in chief, Danielle Wright, almost never told me no, regardless of how odd the story was. "Just go write it, and we'll find space for it. Just don't make it too long," Danielle and Dr. White would say to me.

While I'd worked on a range of pieces—from how students made money as party promoters to how a nineteen-year-old private dancer had found herself dancing in the homes of very powerful state politicians and university professors—the assignment I enjoyed most was writing album reviews. I had a ravenous appetite for music and was at the mall every other week buying new CDs. Considering all of the clothing and food that I was stealing at the time, music somehow was the one thing I always took pride in paying for. Even if I bought the bootleg to get an early listen, I still would turn around and buy the actual album when it was eventually released.

I was glad to pay because I loved hip-hop and I loved writing. Everyone from Outkast to Jay-Z to Trick Daddy Dollars to Master P to Mystikal and Mia X, I reviewed them all. I took my work seriously because I knew that students were deciding how to spend their hard-earned money, and I wanted my words to mean something. I would analyze an artist's lyrics and describe their sound the way a chef would describe flavor when a morsel of food touches their tongue. Coming off of my suspension and finally back in college in the fall of 1999, I focused on album reviews as a way to get my foot back in the door journalistically.

Around the same time, I was working at a Black-owned radio station that had just come on the airwaves, WVHT HOT 105.7. It hadn't been an easy job to get. I had waited too long to get an internship at the campus radio station, and it is very hard to find an off-campus journalism internship when you are actively on probation.

Thankfully, HOT 105.7 was run by Vann and Von Wilson. They were the sons of one of my professors, Dr. Roosevelt Wilson. Professor Wilson knew my father and had a lot of respect for him. I don't think he was ever impressed by me—I never did better than a C in any of his classes—but still he never gave up on me. So on his recommendation, his sons hired me to be the news guy for their hip-hop morning show, *The Breakfast Buffet.* I would ride my bike to that radio station at 5:00 in the morning and pick up a dozen Krispy Kreme doughnuts as instructed along the way. I rode the bike with one hand while balancing a dozen doughnuts with the other, and I walked right in the door to pull the news of the day off of the Associated Press wire site. I made my selects and wrote my copy, and by 6 A.M. I was on the air doing my first of eight news reads for the morning. The only thing missing was a first-grade child at my feet under the desk waiting for me to slap a Hardee's biscuit out of his mouth.

I did this every morning while taking a full load of classes and working at Golden Corral at night and still doing open-mic comedy on the weekends. This earned me the respect of a man who deejayed in the afternoons, DJ Dap. Dap was one of the more prominent and popular DJs in the city. When I had time, he allowed me to sit in on his afternoon drive show and look at how he ran the show: how to work the control board, the order in which he chose to play songs, why he chose that order, how he interacted with the callers, and how he handled the fast-paced nature of radio interviews when artists came in the studio.

This is where I met TJ Chapman.

Today, TJ has managed music artists, run a record label, helped break new music, and established deep roots within the hip-hop community. He is a silent giant who has long been a tastemaker and culture shifter in the music industry. But when I met him in 1999/2000, TJ Chapman was the head of TJsDJs, a major DJ organization that also ran a big record pool. In those days before streaming, when music was a lot more analog than it is now, DJs from across the country would gather from time to time to introduce one another to songs that were hot in their region. They would essentially bring new music, "pool" it together, and all leave with one another's tracks.

It just so happened that Tallahassee was the epicenter of one of the most important record pools. Every three months, TJ Chapman would set up an exclusive music conference at The Moon, an enormous and popular nightclub. It was an exclusive event, and it was always packed. You had a better chance of getting free Super Bowl tickets than you did getting into the TJsDJs Record Pool.

As these top southern DJs mingled around the club drinking and catching up with their friends, some of these new tracks would play, and periodically during the evening, new artists would perform on stage. And it wasn't just DJs in the crowd. There were record label reps, A&R people, radio station DJs and program directors, agents, talent managers, show bookers, and more. The room was *stuffed* to the brim with kingmakers. This was the kind of event that could change your career overnight.

This quarterly meeting was where DJs came to be infected by the next viral record.

Long gone were the days of DJs swapping heavy vinyl records or rickety cassette tapes. TJ's team made sure everyone attending left with a grab bag full of CDs that contained not only the music playing in the club that night but also regional hits from all over the country that hadn't broken out nationally yet. The easiest way for a song to go from being a local hit to a regional hit to a national hit was to get that song in the hands of other DJs at this conference. And the easiest way to get that song in the hands of those DJs was to have your track on one of the CDs in that grab bag.

Every DJ that came to the quarterly meeting would return home and presumably play some of the music from the grab bag in his market. This was the premier way for music to travel from city to city. If your song made it into the bag, it was believed to be a bona fide potential hit. A DJ would listen to it with a more critical ear than if you had simply handed that same track to him on a demo CD at a nightclub on some random night.

TJ also had a record label, Wildstyle Records. And like any good label CEO he made his rounds to all the hip-hop stations to maintain relationships. I came in the studio one afternoon and there sat TJ talking to DJ Dap.

TJ was pretty cool. We talked a little bit about what he did, and eventually we got on the topic of music. The more we talked, the more he could tell that I had a deep appreciation for hip-hop. I explained that I loved listening, not only to a song's radio version, but also to its instrumental track, so that I could really evaluate the song's production. In those days, a song would not only be played on the radio but also sold as a single separate from the album, and on that CD there would usually be an instrumental version or a remix of the song.

I told him that I wrote album reviews for *The Famuan,* and one of his eyebrows shot up. He reached down into one of his bags where he had a few CDs. He handed one to me.

It was for a new artist on his label who he was trying to jump-start some things for. The dude's name was Total Kaos. I had never heard of him, but to hear TJ talk about him, you'd have thought he was the third coming of Jay-Z, Scarface, and Master P.

"He got the goods, man," TJ said. "Trust me."

In a matter of minutes, this man had kind of gone from just being chill to looking at me like I was exactly the person he needed to be talking to today. He didn't bribe me. He simply said, "I can tell that you listen to music in a way where you are going to be fair. Just do me a favor, man, if you can. Listen to the album and just speak your honest opinions."

I'm not even sure I'd bought into Total Kaos as an artist as much as I had bought into TJ Chapman as a person.

TJ continued, "You really would be doing me a solid if you

would just consider reviewing the album. Even if you hate it, man, just write a review for me."

I had known this man all of fifteen minutes and he was talking about this artist, and asking me to review this album, with the conviction of someone making a deathbed wish. I respected it.

The thing that was interesting about the record industry was that TJ knew he wasn't immune from the rules. He could not cheat his own system. If he believed in Total Kaos so much, why didn't he just let him perform on the showcase that *he* set up? Because TJ knew that wasn't enough. You still needed the streets to be buzzing about an artist. Reviews help make that happen.

A review from my paper might lead to a review in another publication, and then another, and before you knew it, DJs would be listening to Total Kaos's records and he would be getting mentioned in the popular music magazines of that time like *Vibe* and *The Source.*

TJ put the album in my hand and I slid it in my backpack. I didn't think anything of it for a couple of days. Then, on a bike ride to campus, I popped it into my CD player and I gave it a listen.

As far as southern rap went, it was fine. There wasn't anything on that album, topic-wise, that wasn't already out there. It had all of the usual braggadocious lifestyle and drugs and violence and death threats that filled most of hip-hop at that time. He had a flow that was unique, and the production was good—that alone is a reason to try something new. But I didn't feel like there was any one track that stood out enough to say, "This guy, for sure, is a clear-cut star who will rise above everyone else in the rap industry." I wrote the review and gave the album a B+.

When the review came out in *The Famuan* a few weeks later, I took an actual hard copy of the paper by TJ's office at his Wildstyle Records recording studio near the edge of town. His store was still a twenty-minute bike ride from the closest bus stop. I was tired and sweaty and just wanted to drop the paper off. TJ unfolded the paper and read the review in front of me, which was pretty nerve-racking, but he seemed to be pleased.

TJ gave me a firm handshake on a job well done.

"Thank you, young brother," he said. "That's some real shit you just did, and I'll never forget it. Let me know if you ever need something."

To which I half-jokingly replied, "A good journalist never takes bribes."

"We'll see," TJ said, smirking.

■ ■ ■

I graduated college a few years later, in 2001, and found myself back home in Birmingham, now interning at WBHJ 95.7 Jamz.

Birmingham was unique in that it was one of the few markets where there were four Black morning shows. The battle for supremacy on morning radio was a constant one. Hometown hero and legendary comedian Rickey Smiley had left big shoes to fill in the morning radio slot. He started on the original hip-hop morning show in the city in 1994 but had since left to host his own morning show in Dallas. I also had to contend with the momentum that Ricky's protégé Ced Delaney had built. You had to come hard. You had to be the funniest. I was also living in the shadows of Alabama comedic behemoths Steve Brown and Sir Walt. It was competitive. You had to be the wildest. You had to be the most daring and then you had to show up tomorrow and do it again.

At 95.7 Jamz, we were irreverent and pushed the envelope. We said all the wrong things for all the right reasons and got laughs. And then when it was time to slow down and be poignant, we did that. Because we showed care and concern for the community, we were given some leeway to be a little edgier from time to time. We were the radio station that started a literal riot after telling people we were going to fly a helicopter over a Walmart parking lot and drop a "million bills." Thousands gathered waiting for their free money and a helicopter indeed flew overhead and dropped one million pictures of former President Bill Clinton. But we were also the radio station responsible for innumerable toy drives and supply drives after house fires and tornadoes.

One thing that I did particularly well was prank phone calls. They weren't my favorite thing to do, but they were a hit on the show and gave me my first real taste of popularity, which in a city like Birmingham was very difficult to accomplish. Birmingham was a tough place. A lot of pain there. Old people carried the scars of the civil rights movement. People my age carried the scars of the war on drugs and the crack era. It took a lot to be able to laugh through some of that.

Four days a week every single week for about four years, I mastered the art of calling up complete strangers and baiting them into becoming enraged with me and cursing me out. It wasn't anything that I pioneered, but I definitely elevated the craft with my contributions. A lot of the times I had been given my targets' information by a family friend who would also suggest an angle of attack guaranteed to upset the person.

But while I was growing in morning radio, I was running into walls within the comedy industry. Even though I'd had a few Black television appearances, including on *Showtime at the Apollo* and BET's *ComicView,* a lot of clubs still refused to book me. Maybe I wasn't their type of comedian, or maybe they had a full roster of guys. But I had a very difficult time playing comedy clubs west of the Mississippi River. Oklahoma City was pretty tough. Houston was really tough. Dallas was impossible. Pretty much anywhere from Dallas up to South Dakota I couldn't get in with.

At the same time, the relationship between stand-up comedians and rappers was catching fire. In the '90s, it wasn't uncommon for a rapper to put a popular stand-up comedian in their music video or in skits on their album. It added a little bit of comedic flair and silliness and entertainment value to the rapper's song and gave the comedian some exposure in the process and an opportunity to co-opt the rapper's fan base.

In the early 2000s, this symbiotic relationship was becoming even more evident. Kanye West employed a lot of Chicago comedians like DeRay Davis on his early albums. Outkast used a few comedians as well, including Birmingham's very own Henry Welch. And also in Atlanta, T.I. had comedians like Kelly "K. Dubb" Walker and Lil Duval as part of his crew popping in and out of his music videos and album sketches.

This got me thinking that TV might not be the only viable medium to reach people. I needed to figure out a way to get my comedy mixed in with their music. If I could get my comedy mixed in with music, then I could get my comedy on the radio. If I could get my comedy on the radio, then local comedy clubs would be more inclined to book me because of my already baked-in fan base.

It's also important to understand that in 2005 the internet was not what it is today. The idea of just videoing yourself and posting a clip of your stand-up comedy was a foreign concept.

I started with the most direct way of reaching radio DJs around the South, which was to simply mail them a demo tape of my prank calls. I told them that the pranks were very funny and it would be an honor if they chose to put them on their mixtapes. All I asked in return was that they give me credit within the album lining and track listings.

I mailed these CDs out to a bunch of radio DJs in cities where I had trouble getting booked.

Crickets.

I couldn't figure out why. From what I could tell, people thought that these prank calls were hilarious.

At the time, I had a prank call that was making its way around the country via email. (Going viral in the early 2000s was essentially sending chain emails to your friends and family.) In "Barbara's

Check," I called a sweet old Black lady and told her that I was a representative of the federal government and that we were cutting her Social Security check and using the money to help with Hurricane Katrina relief. This was an extremely tense issue at the time, because in the months after Hurricane Katrina devastated New Orleans, many New Orleanians were displaced to various southern cities, including Birmingham.

This sudden influx of tens of thousands of people had stressed the local economy and resources. As much as there was sympathy for the hurricane victims, there was also a degree of hostility directed toward them, because people felt like the needs of the refugees were being prioritized over the needs of locals who had far deeper roots.

So, to call a woman and tell her that we were cutting her Social Security check to help this group of people was the powder keg we needed. As with 90 percent of the prank calls that I did, I was asked to do this one by someone close to the person we were pranking. That way at the end of the prank call we had a degree of protection from a backlash. Barbara (like most people I pranked) was a great sport about it and we had a great laugh.

It was by far the biggest and most viral prank phone call I ever did. The call also possessed something else: relatability. Many people in cities that were hosting displaced Katrina survivors had similar mixed emotions about the influx. The prank call touched a nerve, and it made us laugh at something that we had all been feeling but had not wanted to acknowledge. To this day, it is probably the single most popular thing I've ever created.

There was nothing hotter than this prank phone call. People who did not know my face knew my voice. So I figured if ever there was a time to leverage this prank to get more comedy gigs, now was the time.

I still couldn't break through with the radio DJs. I tried everything. I wrote letters. I wrote cover letters. I included color photos. I included printed pictures of the forwarded email chains as a way of proving that people liked me.

Crickets.

I had to figure out another way.

So I called TJ Chapman. I hadn't spoken to TJ since the day I'd dropped off the Total Kaos album review at his offices. We got on the phone and I told him I had a hilarious comedy sketch that would fit perfectly in the CD grab bags he gave DJs at his record pool meetings.

Before I could finish my sentence, TJ cut me off. "The Record pool conference is tomorrow night, so if you trying to get something in for this quarter, you have to come play that for me tomorrow in Tallahassee."

To which I lied and said, "It just so happens that I'll be there tomorrow. I'm um, passing through for a gig in Orlando." I had no gigs in Florida that month, but I needed to meet with him while at the same time I was trying to not seem desperate, even though I really was.

"Boom," he said. "See you then."

The next morning I hopped in the car and drove five hours from Birmingham to Tallahassee solely to play this prank call for TJ Chapman.

Love or hate my stand-up, no one had a bad thing to say about this prank phone call. It was funny. It was topical. It was Black humor at its finest, yet also relatable to white people. It was gold. Without a doubt, TJ Chapman would listen to this record, love it, and allow me to include it in his DJ gift bags.

When I came in the room, TJ was there with about ten or fifteen people. Studio sessions are weird because you can never tell who is the rapper, who is the engineer, and who is the weed guy. Everybody looked and dressed the same. They were in the middle of mixing an album and clearly had been at it for hours. A lot of guys in the room treated my appearance as an opportunity to take a quick five-minute break.

I handed TJ the CD. He popped it into the deck and cranked it. The prank call began to play, and at the parts where most people would already be at least smirking, TJ was expressionless. If TJ refused to laugh, then everyone else in the room refused to laugh too. Nobody wanted to go against the godfather.

The prank call played and played. TJ stared and stared. The more he stared, the more I shrank, to the point where it was embarrassing to be in the room. Oddly, bombing in front of twenty people at point-blank range was far worse than getting booed by thousands at the Apollo. This was my one opportunity, and I could see it evaporating away.

The prank call concluded. TJ took a deep breath and looked over at me and simply said, "Yeah, man. I don't get it. That was not funny to me." My heart sank through the floor. I guess I was supposed to just turn around and leave. But I had come too far, driven too far.

"Yeah, I can see, I can understand that," I said, quivering, "but a lot of people are fucking with it right now. I think it's hot and I think that a lot of people would get it."

TJ paused, like a father contemplating how to not break his child's heart.

He took another deep breath and said, "This isn't funny to me. I don't laugh at stuff like this. I could see why some people think this is funny, but I don't like prank phone calls. I don't like sketches and skits. I've never laughed at any of this shit." My head sank as TJ took yet another breath and continued, "But if you believe that somebody will like this, then you can go ahead and put these in the grab bags."

I was thrilled but still dealing with the sting of embarrassment and couldn't show it. The grab bags were already at the club, which meant I'd have to add my CDs myself. I showed up at The Moon nightclub that night with about ninety demo CDs in hand. Each CD had five or six prank phone calls, and a card inside that invited DJs or rappers to put them on any album for free, in exchange for them giving me credit, by name, on their projects.

While people flirted with one another, while people drank and smoked and engaged in business and casual conversation, I fever-ishly snaked around that nightclub putting my CD into any grab bag that I saw, knowing that some of these bags would end up in the hands of powerful people in music.

A few months later, I got a phone call from a friend in Texas, who simply held his phone up to the speaker. And in the speaker, my prank phone call was playing. Popular Houston rapper Chamil-lionaire had somehow gotten ahold of my CD and had included some of my prank phone calls in his hit mixtape series called "The Mixtape Messiah."

Chamillionaire doing this encouraged another local Houston record label to include my prank phone calls on a series of compila-tion CDs that they were releasing, featuring artists like Bun B and Pimp C of UGK, as well as 8Ball and MJG.

The clout that I received from those two projects was enough to get any and every radio DJ that I'd contacted to start playing my prank phone calls during their shows. This gave me the leverage I needed to get my prank phone calls on independent morning shows and markets where I was not booked.

By the spring of 2006, my prank phone calls were airing not only in Birmingham but in more than fifty different markets across America. Miami, Phoenix, San Francisco, I had every time zone covered. And having a radio presence in multiple local markets was more valuable than any television credit. If my prank phone calls were playing in a city, I could get booked in any comedy club there.

I didn't realize it at the time, but this was the first time I had real proof that I had an audience. My prank phone calls garnered me work in about fifteen new cities over the course of the next two years. This was fucking huge.

The night that I put the CDs in the grab bags, TJ was backstage running the conference, so I never got a chance to tell him thank you. And because I'm not in the world of music, and I rarely played Tallahassee in the years that followed, he and I never crossed paths.

Then one day in 2017, I was in Los Angeles for a gig and decided to run down to Roscoe's Chicken'n Waffles in Hollywood. As I hopped out of my Uber and walked toward the restaurant, there he was, TJ Chapman. He always remembered me, but I don't think he ever remembered or realized how much his keeping his word contributed to my growth.

I didn't do what I did for him with the expectation of a favor in return, but when I needed one, he delivered. Son, it's a lesson I still think about today. We stood there for about fifteen minutes, baking in the California sunlight, as I walked him through the cause and effect of his actions.

He's a humble guy, and he just said, "I respected the fact that you drove five hours on one day's notice just to let me hear that. Sometimes it's not about believing in the product, it's about believing in the person." We shook hands and went our separate ways and that was that.

He still doesn't fuck with prank phone calls.

CHAPTER 14

Keeping the Lights On

E arly one morning, my mother burst into my room.

"That fat motherfucker broke my couch!"

It was 2002. I'd just graduated from college a year earlier. My mom was still in that small nine-hundred-square-foot two-bedroom apartment she moved into after I left for college in 1996.

"Don't just lay there! Come look at my fucking couch!" she again ordered. I slowly crawled out of my childhood twin bed and took a few steps into the living room.

The couch in question was one of the few things belonging to my dad that the IRS decided they didn't want to seize. My father somehow had gotten ahold of it after his mother passed and it had stayed with him ever since. It was light pink and embroidered with all kinds of patterns in the armrests and cushions. Beautiful designs were carved into the wood legs and trim. It was an antique for sure, made in the 1930s or '40s—the kind of couch that belonged in the lobby of a hotel that wouldn't allow Sammy Davis Jr. to stay there.

Approaching the couch, I noticed it was leaning to the side, like a car riding on a donut spare tire. One of the wooden legs of the couch was splintered and crushed. It almost looked like it had exploded. Only something with a ridiculous amount of weight could have done this. My mother was right, that fat motherfucker *did* break her couch. The fat motherfucker in question was my friend, and a fellow comedian, Spanky D. Spanky had a big heart. The only thing bigger than his heart was his size. He was maybe six foot even, but well over three hundred pounds.

"My bad, Mom. I'll see if he can get it fixed."

My mother was more amused than upset. I think she was ready to get rid of that couch anyway. It was a reminder of a time and place and a person that I'm sure she had conflicted feelings about.

Spanky's physique suggested that he could have been a football lineman, but his walk was so smooth you would have been quicker to guess that he was a retired soul singer like Gerald Levert or Barry White. His XXXL suit jackets with matching crewneck T-shirts and cigars would have only solidified your guess. He moved slow and smooth like an aircraft carrier, and if provoked he packed a punch like one as well. Spanky had a deep gruff voice like a blues singer from the Mississippi Delta. He sounded like the old men from Clarksdale who would come to my maternal grandmother's house and buy bags of pecans.

Spanky was twenty years older than me, but in terms of stand-up he'd only been doing the job about three to four years longer. The night before the death of the pink couch, he was passing through Birmingham on the way to another gig and asked to sleep on my couch. It's a common request of one road comic to another—gigs pay shit at the beginning of your career, so if you dare to get a hotel room on an off night, you'll be lucky to break even. But it's somewhat less common when said comic has moved back in with his mother. Still, other comedians had allowed me to sleep on their couches, so I felt it my duty to pay it forward to Spanky.

I got the request cleared with my mom and he came over. At

some point during the night while we were sleeping, our beloved segregation-era couch broke under Spanky's large frame. He was out the door before my mother or I woke up that morning. He was kind enough to leave a note on the kitchen table.

Sorry 'bout that, Dr. Wood, I'll get you another couch.

During the first ten years of my career, I worked with Spanky more than any other comedian. Probably every five to six weeks, I was on a show with him somewhere in the Southeast. If my career was on first base, Spanky's was on second. I paid close attention to his critiques of the industry and which comedy club bookers were doing what to whom. If there was a booker who was bullshit, or if there was a club that I should or shouldn't work, Spanky was always quick to share. He knew which clubs paid on time and which clubs would bounce checks.

Despite our age difference, our styles complemented each other pretty well. I was the young, know-nothing twenty-something fresh out of college. Spank was the military veteran who used humor to escape the pain and horrors of war and, worse, the horrors of divorce. Both were battle experiences he knew all too well. If I was the frantic musician on drums or trumpet, then Spanky and his comedy was a smooth and steady upright bass.

A big reason why I enjoyed working with Spanky was that unlike most other older comedians that I opened for, he never treated me like a child. He treated me like a colleague. He didn't once assume that because I was young I didn't know anything.

One thing that Spanky and I always commiserated about was the need to get a television appearance to solidify our résumés and open up more career opportunities. In the early 2000s, television was the ticket to success and exposure. You needed to be seen performing on a late-night television program, be it Jay Leno, David Letterman, Comedy Central, or BET's *ComicView*. Once you crushed on one of those shows, bookers and agents would be lining up to help you get a TV show or movie.

Of all the TV credits you could gun for as a Black comic, *ComicView* was the easiest to land because they employed the most comedians. By my estimate about 150 to 200 comics were booked each year for the weeknight comedy showcase program. But if *ComicView* had the most slots, it was also the most convoluted to be chosen for. At least with Leno and Letterman you knew who the booker was. It was just a matter of performing in front of that person at a comedy club and then getting a "yes" or "no" that night.

With *ComicView* you sent in a tape and had no idea who would watch it. Some comedians were selected without even sending a tape, because they'd done the show before or were friends of the producers. If you didn't get picked, you could become one of the alternates who sat in the lobby of the theater on the day of taping, hoping one of the booked comedians wouldn't show up. If this happened, a producer scrambled into the lobby looking for anyone they could find.

In terms of its cultural impact, *ComicView* was a far cry from *Def Comedy Jam,* but it was still a respected television credit, and an appearance forced bookers to pay you more on the road. There was no better opportunity to increase your visibility nationally than on BET. You had to have this credit.

My chances of getting selected were low. I didn't play enough Black rooms to build good rapport with the more established Black comedians who were in the producers' inner circle. But every year, like every other Black comic with a dream, I mailed an audition tape to BET. And every year that BET rejection letter came for me like a W-2 during tax time. First there'd be a paragraph of fluff before they dropped the hammer on me in the second paragraph.

"Thank you so much for submitting. Unfortunately your entry was not selected for . . ."

I'd ball the letter up and throw it in the trash before I could even finish it.

In spite of my frustration, year after year, Spanky made sure I submitted. And year after year, it drove me up the wall that I wasn't given an opportunity. I watched every episode and listed every joke that was made and every topic that was broached on the show.

It became easy to predict where jokes were going to go, which gave me the ability to guess with decent accuracy the point of view that most Black comics would *not* have on a topic. These years of angrily watching *ComicView* were the beginnings of what I hoped for my comedy to be. *Even if I'm not the funniest,* I thought to myself, *I'm going to have the freshest perspective.*

Then one year, the next best thing to getting *ComicView* happened to me. Spanky got *ComicView.*

"Yeah, nigga! We going to New Orleans."

I could hear the grin emerging on his face.

"Should we fly or should we drive?"

I sat in silence.

He repeated it.

I finally responded.

"I did not get it this year."

"Man, *fuck* them stupid-ass BET niggas! Them niggas just booking five different versions of the same comedian!"

Even if that was the truth, it didn't take away the pain that I hadn't been selected. I tried as best I could not to be a wet blanket on his moment. I imagined this must be what it felt like to be a minor league baseball player and hear that your teammate had gotten called up to the big leagues.

A few months later my mother saw Spanky on TV.

"You tell that fat motherfucker he owe me a couch," was all she said.

■ ■ ■

As expected, after his *ComicView* episode aired, Spanky started booking gigs in new cities and making more money on the road.

Things were picking up for him, but probably not fast enough to save his marriage. An incident a year or two after New Orleans stands out the most.

Spanky called me one morning. "Hey, little nigga, come drive me down to Cocoa Beach. New room opening up down there, I will put you on stage before me and make sure them white folks put a few dollars in ya pocket."

People with no car always make it sound like you're getting a bargain by being their driver. They say things like "Baby, come scoop me so I can keep you company and you won't drive off the road." Or "Come pick me up and drive me around, and I'll make sure you don't get sleepy." Or "Gimme a ride, I got the weed."

I don't think I ever met another road comedian with worse luck with cars than Spanky. Every time I saw him he had a different car, and every car had a different problem. I don't think he ever had a truly reliable vehicle.

One year it would be a Cutlass, the next it would be a Buick, the year after that it would be a Cadillac but with the door from a Buick. He spent more time at AutoZone than at the comedy club. Every seven or eight months it was an alternator, or a carburetor, or a cracked head gasket, or some other wild repair that literally would cost the exact amount of money that he had gotten paid that week.

I agreed to Spanky's offer to open for him and to drive. Rather than do the entire drive in one day I opted to split the drive to Florida by crashing at Spanky's place in Augusta, Georgia. We'd go the rest of the way the next day. I arrived at Spanky's place late Thursday night. It was a quaint, two-bedroom apartment in a typical southern complex that he shared with his wife. I had met his wife only once or twice before—she didn't come around the comedy shows that much. Most women with careers aren't clamoring to stay with their man in a shitty hotel in middle America. As far as I could tell, most comedians had spouses that were either never around or around far too much—no real in-between. Spanky's appeared to be the former.

It was about 11:00 P.M. or so when Spanky answered his door and ushered me in. He had a couch, but it was pretty sturdy. No way my midtwenties frame was going to break this one. Payback would have to wait.

I settled in and fell asleep.

Around three in the morning I was awakened to the sound of arguing. *Loud* arguing—one of those blowouts that I could tell had simmered for weeks. The louder she yelled, the softer Spanky spoke.

"Where is the fucking money, Spanky?"

"It's going to come in, I'm telling you. I just need a little more time, just give me some time."

"They're going to cut off our fucking lights tomorrow! This is not what I signed up for."

I couldn't tell if this was how Spanky always handled conflict or if he was being on his best behavior because I was in the next room. He stood tall, taking blow after blow. Spanky let her blow off steam, and then took a deep breath.

"The lights are not going to get cut off. I booked those shows tomorrow. When I get the money from those shows, I will wire you the money and we can pay the bill. I know we have been living on the edge, but things take time."

She continued, and from what I deciphered from the argument, she was just a woman who was tired of being broke in a house that was broke. She wanted Spanky to be able to be a provider and uphold his obligations as a man, and maybe somewhere along the line she'd thought stand-up comedy would be far more linear as a career. But that's the interesting thing about stand-up. The money may come in year three, the money may come in year twenty, or the money may never come, but you have to stay at the table and continue to roll the dice, hoping that your number hits. Spanky's wife was ready to leave the casino.

The other thing about stand-up comedy is, once you've been in the casino too long, you really can't go back out into the regular world because there aren't many other jobs that you are qualified to do.

I won't judge the totality of a couple's marriage on one 3 A.M. argument. Knowing what I know now about stability and what most women expect from men in a relationship, there's no question: Spanky wasn't meeting her needs, and I am sure he was fully aware of that.

The next morning, I was awakened by the sound of dishes clanking and eventually the smell of bacon. The easiest way to rouse a southerner is the smell of breakfast. Spanky's wife had laid out a pretty palatial spread for the two of us. We filled up on bacon, biscuits, and cheese grits, and then we hit the road.

Spanky didn't talk much about the argument in the car. It seemed like he wanted to forget it. But he did say that money problems were stressing his relationship a great deal.

The ride from Augusta to Cocoa Beach, Florida, was otherwise uneventful until just south of Jacksonville, Florida, when we got a phone call from Larry. Larry was a booker of a few mid-major comedy clubs in Florida along the East Coast. He didn't own his own brick-and-mortar building—most of his comedy club rooms were in rented-out hotel lounges and restaurants. They weren't the greatest venues, but they weren't nearly the worst. Considering that Florida had some of the highest volume of stage time in the country, some of the clubs were bound to be mediocre.

You could be performing in a retirement home one night and the patio of a sushi restaurant the next, and less than two miles up the road you could be performing on the beach.

Because of this volume, comedy club owners in Florida were very territorial. There was a bit of a gentleman's agreement among all of them that they wouldn't try and start a room within a certain amount of miles of some else's club. That "respect radius" varied depending on the booker and on the city.

If a booker barged into some else's territory, then the aggrieved booker would threaten to ban any comedians who worked the new room. The fear of being blacklisted restricted the talent pool that the new comedy club could recruit from, essentially suffocating the new room out of the market. But this rule only worked if the comedians complied and did not work the new room.

Unbeknownst to Spanky and myself, Larry had taken great offense to us being the debut comics for this new club in Cocoa Beach that was apparently opening a little too close to his more established club. As my Ford Focus zoomed down I-95 south of Jacksonville, the fireworks began.

Larry called me first. He didn't know I was in the car with Spanky. I put the call on speakerphone, partly because I was driving but also because I wanted Spanky to hear the conversation.

"Roy, not cool. Roy. Not cool," Larry began.

I had only worked for Larry once before, and that gig was me covering for another comedian who had canceled on him at the last minute. He'd never booked me outright.

"Um, hey Larry, what can I do for you?" I cautiously responded.

It was for sure odd that he was calling me. With the pleasantries out the way, Larry revved up the pace of the conversation. It wasn't so much us having a conversation as it was me being given a chance to just shut up and listen to him talk.

"Roy, I understand that you and Spanky are about to perform in a new room that's up the street from my spot. It'd mean a lot to me if you didn't do that. I have done a lot of hard work to establish comedy in this town, and this new guy is just coming in and trying to steal my customers. It's not right and they do comedy wrong. People will go over there, see terrible comedy in a terrible room, and lose faith in the artform, and then both rooms will close."

I sat in silence deciding how to respond and Spanky bit his lip like a ferocious dog begging to be let off the leash. I was young and naive and believed the lie that people like Larry sold new comedians. They'd tell you that they were piped into Hollywood and that your relationship with them would make or break your chances of having real opportunities in the industry.

I timidly explained to Larry that the booker I worked for had been kind to me and given me regular work. I didn't see why I shouldn't be allowed to perform at the new room in Cocoa Beach, especially considering that Larry didn't book me himself.

"You need to learn rules to this shit, kid," Larry snapped back. "That guy is a snake."

I kept my cool and told Larry I'd think about it. As soon as I hung up the phone, Spanky's phone rang. Spanky put him on speakerphone.

"Hey, Spanky, it's Larry. I know you are doing that gig in Cocoa Beach tonight. What you need to understand is, that restaurant has stolen the exact layout of my show. I spoke with Roy and he has already said he isn't going to do the show. I'm hoping you'll extend me the same courtesy."

The entire time, Spanky grinned.

"Look, man, you ain't never worked me. I gotta chase you for work," he said. "What you gon' do? Ban me from the rooms that you already don't work me in? You must be a stupid motherfucker. Nigga, fuck you for even calling."

Then he hung up in his face.

Most comedy club bookers, especially ones that book small one-nighters, are fucking liars and thieves. They overcharge the venue for the talent, and then they underpay the talent and pocket most of the cash. There was a guy who booked comedy in a hotel in central Florida who would pay the headliner $150 and pay the feature act $75. We found out years later that he was charging the hotel $2,000 a week to book comedy. And *on top of that,* he was taking a

10 percent booking fee from the comedians that he was booking for the room that he was already getting overpaid from. "Nigga, please" indeed.

The South was littered with these types of motherfuckers, and the more Spanky explained that to me as we rode down the freeway, the less guilty and nervous I felt about my decision to simply say, "I'll think about it."

About fifteen minutes later, my phone rang. It was Larry again.

"Look, man, you're a very funny comedian. I have not done a good job of booking you. So, how about this—what do you say right now I open up my calendar and I give you four weeks of feature work?" As he said this, Spanky motioned for me to mute the call.

"He'll give you the dates, then cancel them next month," Spanky said. "Fuck him."

I unmuted the phone.

"I can't do that. I've already counted this money into my finances," I said. "Also, I don't want to cancel on someone the day of the show. So, how about this? How about I do this show, and I will give you my word that I will never perform there again, provided you give me some dates?"

Larry went on a long rant about loyalty and how it was time that I scratch his back. Bookers have a way of feeding you scraps, but when they need something from you, they want to remind you of all of the filet mignon they have given you. I heard him out and told him that my position respectfully stood. He hung up in my face.

Two seconds later, Spanky's phone rang again. Larry again told Spanky that I'd dropped out of the show and he would give Spanky two weeks of headline work right now if he dropped out too. Spanky thought about it for literally half a second.

"Pay me in full for both gigs, right now today via wire transfer, and I'll cancel on this—"

"You motherfucking comedians are so fucking ungrateful, and you don't fucking realize the battle we fight to establish comedy in all of these cities for you," Larry said. "In two years, there will be no comedy in Cocoa Beach and it'll be your fault, you motherfucker."

Spanky hung up in his face.

I sat there stunned. I'd never seen anybody stand up to authority like that before. I'd never seen anybody so casually not even consider the consequences of choosing to be a man. I was young, and I wasn't nearly as bold in how I handled conflict, and it was very empowering to see.

"None of these motherfuckers hold the keys to what you are trying to do," Spanky said. "Don't ever be afraid to walk away with no check. If you got talent, you gon' get opportunities. Don't let these bookers tell you how you should and shouldn't be making money. Fuck that motherfucker. If he liked us so much, he should have been breaking bread. Ain't nobody who ain't putting money in my pocket ever gon' tell me how the fuck I should be making moves. He shouldn't even be calling my motherfucking phone. If you ain't putting money in my pocket, love in my heart, or pussy in my face, you can't tell me how to make moves."

We laughed so hard we had to pull over at a truck stop to take a piss.

I got back to the car and saw three missed calls from the booker of our comedy show. Also unbeknownst to me and Spanky was the fact that Larry was kind of *the man* in Cocoa Beach. Apparently, someone—no clue if it was Larry himself—had purchased one of those big sandwich board signs and stood in front of our comedy venue telling everyone that the comedy at this place was terrible and to not come to the show tonight. At the same time, someone—again, no clue if it was Larry—had made a couple calls down to the liquor board, and the restaurant's liquor license had been temporarily suspended while the liquor board double-checked their compliance.

A lunatic standing in the Florida heat wearing a sandwich board is one thing, but someone taking away your ability to make money off drinks is another. It was enough for the restaurant to call off our show. To his credit, the booker of our show tried everything he could to convince the venue to at least honor that night's show, but they were too scared of Larry.

Feeling sympathetic for us, our booker agreed to pay us half the money we were owed, but it would be via check and would take at least a week to get to us. This meant Spanky wouldn't have the money for the power bill tonight. We sat in silence as the slow rumble of an eighteen-wheeler passing by shook the car.

I understood Spanky's predicament. It's one thing to lose the money, but it's another to have to go back home to your wife and tell her that you've lost the money. The laughs we'd been sharing were completely vacuumed out of the car.

After about ten minutes, Spanky mumbled in a barely audible tone, "Man, take me home. Just take me home." I started up the Ford Focus and off we went.

Back on the freeway, we just sat in silence. No radio, no music, no satellite radio comedies, just the silent roar of the freeway. Spanky began to weep softly. It wasn't loud. It wasn't howling. It was the soft, silent crying of a man who was tired of having life do this to him, and who had to tell his wife that their power was going to get disconnected.

I guess I'm lucky I've never been with a woman who was impatient, but I've also been fortunate to date women whose expectations of me matched where I was in my career at the time.

Spanky and I didn't say a word to each other. When we got back to Savannah, it was clear that he did not want to go in that house. I pulled over at a bank.

I had exactly $240 to my name, and I withdrew it. I kept $40 for gas to get me home and I gave the other $200 to Spanky. Not enough to save his power bill, but it was better than nothing.

When we got to his house, he jokingly suggested, "You're more than welcome to come back in and spend the night."

"No, thanks," I said. "I'd rather fall asleep on the road and crash into some shit."

There is a scene in *Kill Bill: Volume 2* where David Carradine's character knows for sure that death is imminent. He knows that the moment he stands up and starts walking, he's going to drop dead from his injuries. Still, he wipes the blood from his mouth, straightens his collar, gets his chin off his chest, and stands up and walks toward his imminent demise. This was the look on Spanky's face as he prepared to face his wife and hit her with the news.

I am not sure what I would've done in that scenario. I also didn't hang around to find out what happened. I was peeling out of that parking lot the second Spanky closed the door. As slow as he was walking, I'm sure I was halfway to Atlanta before he walked in that house.

Spanky and his wife's marriage didn't last too long after that, maybe a couple of years. But after their divorce, I distinctly remember the freedom in Spanky's face as we went from gig to gig. I saw him less and less over the years as I started to become a headliner myself. You don't run into comedians of equal ability too often, but every blue moon, we'd end up in the same town or get booked for the same comedy festival, and the times I saw him, Spanky was jubilant. Optimism radiated from his pores no matter the circumstances.

Neither of us was rich, and we were still pretty much struggling gig-to-gig to pay our bills, even after all that time. But there was a freedom to him. He never seemed stressed.

When you have a job that's not linear, like being a comedian, you have a responsibility to inform the people who attach themselves to you exactly what this life is all about. I'll never know whether Spanky sold his wife the dream, but I did learn from him that as an entertainer, if someone falls in love with you, it's not your job to sell them the dream, it's your job to sell them the nightmare.

Selling the nightmare is how you will find the people who love you or how you'll decide that you're better off alone. You can't be in a relationship with someone who doesn't understand why you are the way you are and who isn't truly serious about being in the mud with you. I'm not saying that that's fair to the person who decides to attach themselves to you, but it's a choice they have to make for themselves. They deserve to make that choice with all the information.

The only person I had better conversations with in the car was my father. Those days and nights on the road with Spanky felt very similar. I can't go in an AutoZone to this day and not think of him.

I wish I could tell Spanky that the feeling of pressure to succeed, the paranoia that it's all going to leave you, never leaves. There's always something new to pay for. You will have to make a choice to either shield the people you fall in love with from this paranoia or bathe them in it. Both have consequences. You can share your fears and the dips in your career roller coaster, but if they don't handle stress as well as you, then their stress can make it harder for you to survive in your industry.

But if you share nothing with them, then you run the risk of being with someone who truly doesn't understand the stress of what you do and just how hard it is to handle it the higher your career climbs. In these types of relationships, you can find yourself feeling underappreciated and eventually resentful of their blindness to the challenges you face.

There is no wrong choice, son. But there probably isn't a right one either. I don't think Spanky's wife was completely wrong. I wish I could tell him that you're never going to meet a woman who's not at some point going to assess your ability to provide, as she should, and that you just have to tell her what she's married to.

Spanky died of a heart attack in 2018. I didn't go to his funeral. I don't really do funerals in general, but I definitely don't do funerals for dead comedians. I would be going to three or four funerals a year if that were the case. There was a GoFundMe digital fundraiser for his burial costs, which I donated to alongside a lot of comedians. Spanky was loved in our community. The target amount of the GoFundMe was well exceeded.

I told my mom how much money Spanky's family raised in his death, to which she calmly mumbled, "See if they got enough money to get me some furniture. That fat motherfucka died before he could fix my couch."

CHAPTER 15

Gotta Know When to Go

He was by far one of the most electric comedians I ever saw. He could go from a simmering, reserved, quiet ball of discomfort in the green room to a supernova of energy and laughs, just by walking onstage. He was the type of comedian who could make you laugh before he even landed at the microphone. Sometimes he'd jump off the stage and gyrate with the audience. He hadn't even opened his mouth and you knew that there was nothing about this show that was going to be typical. There was nothing about him that you had ever seen before.

One time he came off the stage and started dry-humping a guy in the crowd whose arm was in a sling. This guy was actively trying to get away from him, and this comedian was only getting closer and closer and throwing his crotch more and more in his face, so much so that the guy fell out of his chair onto the shoulder in the sling.

Of course, every comedian in the room was thinking, *Who the fuck has shoulder surgery and then goes out for drinks?* And I'm sure that guy was thinking, *Who the fuck comes off the stage and throws their dick in your face like a fucking Luther Campbell Miami twerk video?* There were points to be had on both sides. The guy sued the club and it had to pay his medical damages for him to have new rotator cuff surgery. Soon after, a policy was implemented: "Under no circumstances is a comedian allowed to leave the stage during their performance." The policy still stands to this day at the Comedy Club Stardome in Birmingham.

After grinding on a random audience member, he'd jump back on stage, take the microphone out of the mic stand, and give the DJ the cut symbol. The music would suddenly stop, giving way to hoots and hollers and yells of approval. He'd stand there with a beaming smile as his chest rose up and down like that of an oxygen-starved gymnast who knows she's just stuck an amazing landing. The man had yet to even take the mic out of the stand or even say hello to the audience yet he stood there basking in his first applause break of the night.

His name was Michael Roof. Stage name: Chicken.

I first ran into Chicken around the Birmingham comedy scene. By the time I started in 1998, he had already headlined shows after doing comedy for only three or four years, which in our business is a relatively short amount of time to go from open mic to headliner. Chicken was a gifted comedian who had great jokes, but more important, he was likable. He had a real southern charm to him. Chicken was not your typical dog-loving, rifle-hunting, slam-a-few-beers-back white southerner. He was the type of white dude who you know could name every Ice Cube and N.W.A track—even their B-sides—but could also do the same for Queen and Guns N' Roses. He could name the starting offensive line for the University of Alabama but could then turn right back around and tell you the item number of some jewelry he saw on QVC. He knew how to relate to anyone and everyone.

In Birmingham he was a legend because he was one of the few

comedians to go from host to headliner. He never featured. This was unheard of.

In a traditional comedy club hierarchy, the host is usually the most novice comic on the bill. Sometimes the host is referred to as the emcee. They do about ten to fifteen minutes of material to get the audience warmed up.

Then there's a featured act who does thirty minutes. The featured act is someone with a lot more experience but not quite enough material or popularity to be able to headline. You could linger in this feature spot in the comedy club world for anywhere from two to ten years. Some comedians never graduate from this level if they aren't inventive enough.

After the feature comes the headliner. Headliners are people with a solid forty-five minutes of material. They're the best performers of the night. Headliners come with varying capabilities. The ability to talk for forty-five to sixty minutes can get you a headlining gig on a Tuesday or Wednesday night when the people are usually in the comedy club for free or on discounted tickets—so that there's no love lost if the show isn't spectacular. But then you have your weekend headliners. They can be anyone from an '80s road dog with three decades in the game, to a rising star comedian with one television credit, to a superstar you just saw in a movie the week before.

The other thing to know about comedy shows is that there should be an escalation in energy as each performer comes to the stage. Club owners work very hard to choose comedians whose styles complement one another, so that the show stylistically flows from one comedian to the next.

In comedy, you pair performers the same way you pair a meal. If you order a steak, you'll probably order some green vegetables and a starch as sides. If you order a slice of apple pie, it wouldn't be unreasonable to add a scoop of ice cream and maybe some cinnamon or whipped cream.

Adding Chicken to most shows was like adding a bowl of spicy chili on top of your meal. His presence was so imposing that he was all you wanted to see, no matter who was on stage later. It doesn't matter what you are eating when you add chili to it—you are now eating chili.

Chicken's act was amazing and electric, but if he worked as an emcee his energy was so unbridled that the feature act could not match it. Comedians who performed after him sometimes struggled to connect with the audience. Very few could match his level of energy. He was so high-octane that anybody who came on stage after him felt like jazz at a heavy metal concert.

The same went for headliners—some refused to work with him if the club had him booked as a host. Chicken was his own thing. He wasn't the opposite of anyone. And there was no diet version of him either. It was like watching Jim Carrey on cocaine and Red Bulls. There was a sprinkle of Chris Farley in there too.

As the legend goes, one night, early in his career, Chicken was booked to emcee but the headliner was unable to make it. It was too close to showtime to get another comedian to come in, so the owner had no choice but to give Chicken and fellow comedian Reno Collier an opportunity to perform a longer set together. They called it "The Chunky Chicken Show."

The duo did their thing headlining together for a few years. If nothing else, that show proved Chicken was ready to headline on his own. He tore the roof off the place. He never featured at the club again. Went straight to headliner after that. This type of shit never happens. It would be like getting drafted into the NBA out of high school, starting, and winning a championship in your first year. Not even Kobe did that.

Not too long after he became a headliner in the mid-'90s, Chicken caught the attention of some major L.A. talent agents and found himself at the Just for Laughs Comedy Festival in Montreal. At the time, Just for Laughs was the premier talent showcase event for performers, comedy's equivalent of the NFL Combine. For two weeks every July the best up-and-coming comedians performed in a series of live shows all over the city attended by tens of thousands of people. Also in the crowd were tons of television agents and movie producers looking to cast the next bright stars in entertainment. If you did well here, there was someone in this crowd who would change your life that weekend.

A lot of the Just for Laughs talent bookers talk to the club owners, watch live shows across the nation, and even look at submission tapes to decide who will get the prestigious slots in the festival. I was fortunate enough to go in July of 2006 and did so well that three months later I performed for the first time in late night on *The Late Show with David Letterman.*

I have no idea why Canada is the place where all of this happens, but my guess is that because Montreal is an international city, the better you do as an American comic with audiences that know little to nothing about America, the more universal appeal you might have.

But that's just speculation.

Chicken went there and crushed. It was the set of a lifetime. Every joke worked. Performances of this magnitude would cause a bidding war between networks to sign talent to a holding deal. This meant that a network had locked you with a set amount of money for a project to be created later, and you could no longer sign with any other networks while at the festival. This number could be anywhere from $50,000 to $500,000.

But at the time, there was also a lot of poaching going on. You could have a killer set on Monday and have a deal in place with ABC on Tuesday, but your agent could bump into an NBC exec on Wednesday and get NBC to double ABC's offer before they could even draw up the contracts. It was cutthroat, it was backstabbing, it was Hollywood at its finest.

After his show, one network was so intent on signing Chicken that they not only paid him—six figures, it's rumored, to keep him from being poached by another network while the contracts were still being drawn up—they also paid him to leave town after his first performance. A few months later, he was awarded a sketch show called *Hype* that would air on the new WB Network that fall.

Chicken accomplished all of this in a very short time. What maybe takes some performers fifteen to twenty years to do, Michael Roof had just done in less than five. To go from emcee to headliner to a six-digit talent deal and your own sketch show is fucking insane.

So when I finally got to open for him one weekend in Birmingham, I was excited. I had only been doing stand-up for about two years. His sketch show on WB had not premiered yet, but they were already in the process of shooting episodes. He talked excitedly about all of his ideas and how great everyone was in L.A. To new comedians, especially in Birmingham, Los Angeles seemed like another world, so to meet anybody who had dared to get on a plane to L.A. was a godsend. You might as well be talking to someone who had visited Mars. Talking to him made me feel like the dream was possible.

Between shows, Chicken and I continued our conversation. He took the opportunity to wipe some sweat from his face and talk excitedly about a war movie he was going to have the chance to audition for. Chicken talked about how pumped he was to have a shot at the film, about his dreams of being a dramatic actor, and that threw me off because this guy had been to the mountaintop of stand-up comedy and he was already thinking about the next mountain that he wanted to climb.

You're the legendary comedian who killed so hard at Montreal that they paid you to leave town and you want to be a *serious* performer too?

I'm grateful that I got to work with Chicken that week in Birmingham, because emcees are sometimes paired with veteran headliners who never really got their shot in Hollywood. Their bitterness fills the green room like the onions in a salad that's been left on the dashboard of a car in the summer. Chicken was a fresh bouquet of optimism. Just as I'd grown up studying the best comedians, he'd grown up studying the best actors, and he dreamed of being among them. It was in those moments that I saw the glimpses of who Michael Roof really was. Chicken was more of a mask, an entry-point character to draw people in. Then, when he had your attention, he'd show you a different, a deeper, a more heartfelt version of himself.

But that night he was chili and I was happy to be the cornbread.

Chicken had this joke about Deion Sanders, who at the time was one of the best cornerbacks in the NFL but at this point was a little later in his career and starting to have some injury issues. He was having repeated issues with turf toe. Chicken took this news on stage and made a meal of it.

"Deion Sanders can't play football this week because he sprained his toe. I thought football players were supposed to be tough. He didn't sprain his toe, he sprained his vagina!"

As the audience cackled, he continued.

"Football players make millions of dollars. I don't care if I lost both of my arms, I would still be out there playing cornerback."

Chicken then put both of his arms inside of his shirt and folded his arms, exposing his elbows through the sleeves and pretending to be a double amputee. He then went from side to side on the stage, simulating defense on an imaginary wide receiver. This joke will never read as hilarious as it was to see, but I assure you, audiences were crying with laughter. That was the magic of who he was. He could take a simple thought and get a chuckle, but he could then perform that thought and create an uproar.

At the end of our gig in Birmingham, we shook hands after a

solid weekend of performing and went our separate ways. *Hype* premiered on the WB Network in October of 2000. The show came and went without much fanfare and was canceled after one season.

But he seemed to be doing okay in films. After all, he wanted people to know Michael, and *Hype* was just a vehicle for Chicken. Turns out that war movie he was auditioning for was the critically acclaimed *Black Hawk Down*, directed by Ridley Scott, which came out in 2001. Not long after, he booked a role alongside Vin Diesel and Samuel L. Jackson in a spy movie called *xXx*. He also popped up again in the sequel. After that, it would be another five or six years before we'd meet for the second and final time.

There used to be a comedy night in a college nightclub in Columbia, Missouri, called Deja Vu. Deja Vu was a traditional college bar/nightclub full of rowdy college kids hopped up on Red Bull and vodka. There was a second club upstairs where they did comedy. The comedy was simply a way to get the coeds riled up before they headed downstairs to dance the liquor out of their system and give each other cold sores. No one in that room was over twenty-five. I was probably the oldest person there, and I was in my late twenties. It was understood that Deja Vu was the type of club where you could probably get some ass after the show if you were lucky. More often than not, comedians after the show would just hang around until someone felt sorry for you and bought you a drink.

But it was generally a club where high-energy acts did well. The crowd was loud, the crowd was raucous. They all had short attention spans, so you needed quick-fire material. One poorly placed joke about police harassment usually had me on everyone's shit list there, and it would take me about ten minutes of drinking jokes to make my way out of that hole. I always had enough jokes to do well as a feature, but as a headliner it took some time for me to be able to kill without touching on topics that turned my set into a political standoff with an audience that just wanted their usual jokes about beer and football and farts.

It was maybe 2008 when I arrived there one week to perform as a feature. I never asked who was headlining during the weeks that I was featuring because I truly did not care. Regardless of who was performing before or after me, my job was to be funny for thirty minutes. Still, I was shocked to find out that the headliner was Chicken. I'm not talking shit about the club, but Deja Vu wasn't exactly the type of comedy spot that someone who's done Vin Diesel movies should be playing anymore. But sometimes comedians are working on new jokes for a comedy special and they deliberately play in smaller markets to get everything tuned up before the bigger markets, so I assumed that was his plan.

As usual, Chicken brought the house down. He even cracked out the old Deion Sanders joke.

Deja Vu did not have a green room. The only place for comedians to tuck off and hide after the show was a storage room behind the bar. The room reeked of cardboard and was filled with the sounds of a carbon dioxide tank extracting soda syrup from the maze of tubes connected to the fountain soda boxes that filled the space. What seemed like endless shelves of bottom-shelf vodka and Rumple Minze and Goldschläger bottles lined the walls. It wasn't comfortable. It was so narrow that you had to stand sideways. But if you wanted solitude from the two stories of laughing, drunk twenty-somethings and pulsating EDM music downstairs, this was the only place to be.

I took a break between shows. I found Chicken there. He had managed to push some of the liquor bottles aside on the shelf to create a makeshift seat for himself.

He had a very distant and dead look on his face. The happiness that had radiated from it in Birmingham a decade earlier was gone. A comedian who did that well on stage would normally be out at the bar enjoying the plethora of free shots that people want to shower you with. Women would ask you to sign their breasts and jockey to see who would give you some ass that night. In my years playing Deja Vu, I have even seen women buy a ticket to the very next show just to sit up front with no panties on and slide their skirts up for the headliner. He could easily be out there in the ruckus enjoying the fruits of his labor.

"I am sick of this shit, bro," he mumbled. "I'm just tired."

I'd opened for many a comedian at this point, and I'd heard all the gripes, so I took it as such. I asked Michael if he had been working on any new material and he said no. He explained that the act that got him to become a headliner so fast was now the only thing that was helping him to pay bills. The acting opportunities were not coming as quickly as he'd hoped.

There's a danger to being a comedian who does a character on stage. If you're not careful, you become a prisoner of that character. The expectations of the audience are for you to be that person, and if you do not have a place to unplug from that, it can be a difficult place to exist. I believe that Chicken was one of Michael Roof's many characters. Chicken was not Michael, but to keep food on the table, Michael had to be Chicken. Knowing what I know now with almost thirty years in the business, Michael's rapid ascent into Hollywood—skipping the feature act level along the way—denied him some of the growing pains necessary for creative exploration and growth. As an emcee you're simply learning how to get comfortable with being on stage. As a feature you're learning how to be comfortable with experimentation and failure. He missed this level.

Those emotional dips are essential for learning who you are and, as Dave Chappelle would say, identifying your joke machines and learning what triggers new ideas within you and how to extract creativity from yourself. Stand-up comedy is a never-ending cycle of "I know what I'm doing" and "Oh my God, what the hell am I doing?" Once you are a movie star, the expectations of the audience prevent you from having the freedom of failure that a stand-up comedian needs to truly evolve.

Michael was back in the clubs performing material that he had already intellectually matured past. I could only imagine what type of prison that must've been. I opted to give him space and relegated myself to a quiet part of the bar playing Golden Tee Golf and foosball with strangers.

The second show went off without a hitch. When it was time to turn it on, Michael Roof turned it on. He gave the audience Chicken, and he gave it to them for forty-five minutes, the same as he had in the Birmingham days. They loved it. He walked off the stage to a roaring ovation and back to the solitude of the supply room. I got a call about a year or so later from a mutual comedian friend telling me that Michael Roof had died by suicide. It was said that he had issues with depression, severe anxiety, and bipolar disorder.

I will never know everything there is to know about why Michael chose to do that. I interacted with him for a total of just two nights in my entire life. There are a ton of comedians who were much closer to him and who could probably give me a window into the complexities of whatever it was he was dealing with. But even if I had that information, it all boils down to speculation, and this is not the place for that. Still, I think about Michael Roof often.

I talked to him only twice, but on two distinctly different parts of his career trajectory. Comedians wear sadness and general disdain on their being the way football players wear grass stains. It's so commonplace it's hard to know when you're looking at someone in deep pain or someone playing the part to belong.

Michael was the first comedian I knew who died this way, which is an odd thing to say. But if you're in entertainment long enough, you're going to accumulate coworkers who die tragically. At publication of this book, I'm at around ten comedians I've known who died by suicide. That number jumps to fifteen once you throw in drug overdoses, and almost twenty-five when you add in bike accidents, car crashes, and medical shit.

Michael Roof is the one who really sticks with me. I wonder if it's because the optimism I saw in him, I see in myself. I dream just as hard. I remember the excitement in his face. This man was going where I one day hoped to go, and he'd returned from that place a shell of himself—saddened and suicidal.

I never once questioned whether I should still go to Los Angeles, but what Michael Roof showed me was that there's an importance to doing something that feeds your soul. I saw his unhappiness in his work with my own eyes. He was dissatisfied with where he was career-wise, and to me he seemed out of ideas on what to do next. It became my greatest fear, and it remains my greatest fear to this day, to live without joy.

■ ■ ■

My memories of Michael Roof are a large part of why I decided to quit *The Daily Show* in 2023. I felt myself becoming unhappy there. I wanted to do more. The more I looked at the logistics of the show, and at the content we were creating versus the content that I was starting to imagine, the more I knew that the things that I wanted to do weren't always going to be of use in that format.

People think that my leaving this show was some sort of power move because I did not feel like I was considered for host after then host Trevor Noah's exit from the seat in 2022. But I really left the job because I was afraid I wouldn't be happy creatively, or would be pushed out by a new host. I left before Jon Stewart was rumored to be returning as a host. The other fear was that I would be a pay cut casualty, because at the time of my departure, Comedy Central's parent company, Viacom/Paramount, was going through a merger. And usually when a big company comes in to take over a smaller television network, there are cuts to staff or entire shows are canceled.

If I stay and then I am forced to leave, will I have as many job opportunities as if I just leave now on my own volition? This was the question.

My mood shift didn't hit me all at once. It had been in years in the making.

I think it started in the summer of 2022 when *The Daily Show* announced that it would be going to Georgia for a week of live shows in Atlanta the week before the midterm elections. In the months leading up to the live shows, every correspondent was encouraged to pitch a story focused on something happening within the state of Georgia. The cool thing about *The Daily Show* is that the best idea wins. Anyone in the building can pitch an idea and watch it trickle up the chain of command. Georgia Week was no different. Correspondents pitched, writers pitched, segment producers pitched, field directors pitched. When the dust settled, about eight to ten stories had made the final list that Trevor and the producers would then whittle down to the four to five stories that would actually be shot.

The irony is that for a comedy show that covers the government, when it's time for the producers to choose a story and a correspondent to assign it to, the building operates very similar to Washington, D.C. A *Daily Show* segment has a better chance of being approved by the higher-ups if there is more than one person vouching for how good it could be. So if you pitched a story, then it was in your best interest to move like a congressman. You'd walk around the building looking for a writer who agreed that your story was great and who would "cosponsor your bill." Then, you and that writer would reach out to a senior producer in the hope that your excited conversation about the idea would be remembered when they got behind closed doors with the powers that be to make a decision.

Having seen how the process generally unfolded once things were down to the final eight to ten stories, I knew for sure I was going to be covering one of two stories. One was pitched by someone else, the other by me.

The two stories were:

COP CITY (SOMEONE ELSE'S PITCH): The City of Atlanta approved the tearing down of a forest to build a multi-million-dollar training facility for police and fire departments, complete with full-size streets and buildings. Opponents of the plan dubbed it "Cop City" and believed it would be a waste of money and an environmental disaster, and that it would train police, not on how to de-escalate situations, but on how to be fiercer. At that time in 2022, construction had yet to begin on Cop City because a series of highly organized protesters were living in the forests and occupying the land that needed to be cleared. Construction had been delayed for well over a year because of their tactics, costing the state valuable time and money. The plan for the story was to go into the forest and talk to the forest defenders, as well as to talk with some Black environmentalists about the long-term impacts of the new watershed that would be created by replacing forest with concrete. Thus leading to more flooding downstream in predominantly Black neighborhoods.

MORRIS BROWN COLLEGE (MY PITCH): An acclaimed historically Black college in Atlanta reopened their doors in 2022 after nearly twenty years of nonexistence. At the time there was a lot of national discourse about the state of Black colleges. Then-president Joe Biden was providing aid to these Black schools, and this was also a few years after then-president Donald Trump had met with the presidents of many of these Black colleges and pledged money as well. I wanted to have a serious conversation with the president of Morris Brown about what I believed to be a bleak future for Black colleges, about whether some Black colleges needed to contract to help others survive, and about the larger question of whether going to college was even still necessary.

Because I had gone to an HBCU, Florida A&M, I had a soft spot in my heart for the plight of Black colleges, which was why I lobbied to get my Morris Brown pitch approved. The challenges facing Black colleges were often a topic of discussion within Biden's administration. Yes, police reform was a major issue, as was the environment, but I felt like any of the correspondents could cover Cop City. I felt like only I could build the trust necessary for having an open and honest conversation about the state of Black colleges with the president of a Black college. My mother and father had also graduated from Black colleges, and my upbringing would give me the runway I needed to fairly criticize how some Black colleges handled their funds, without the interviewee getting offended and treating me as an outsider.

Also, the Cop City story was already national news because one of the forest protesters had died in a shootout with the police. This story was not going anywhere, and we could cover it any time before or after we left Atlanta. However, our Georgia live show would probably be the only time we could justify doing a story about a shutdown Black college that was struggling to get back on its feet, Morris Brown College. To me, it was either now or never for this story.

I gently pressed my department heads and their department heads. Everyone understood why the story was important to me, but in the end I lost that battle and was sent to Atlanta to cover Cop City instead of Morris Brown. They argued that if the force defenders were able to stave off construction of Cop City, then maybe they would offer a game plan for success to protesters in other states where similar facilities were being built. Essentially, Cop City was a local story with more immediate national consequences. Morris Brown was not. I couldn't argue this counterpoint.

I was reassured that we'd get to the Morris Brown story down the road, but deep down I knew that the story was dead.

After the COVID-19 pandemic, correspondents went out for

field pieces less frequently, which meant that stories we were getting sent out for couldn't always be the interesting niche stories. The stories had to connect to a larger piece of a national puzzle.

In the new media landscape, your stories had to touch on issues that people were already talking about, and if there was one thing people were *not* talking about on a national level, it was the fiscal crisis that was happening at our Black colleges. I understood but still oddly found myself disappointed.

It's not like the piece I was being sent out to cover wasn't still going to tell the story of discrimination against Black people. The areas that would be flooded when Cop City was completed were predominantly Black. The people who will be harassed by these new policing tactics would be predominantly Black. And I had been given ample runway in my eight years at *The Daily Show* to tell uniquely Black stories, from covering the twentieth anniversary of the Million Man March to Chicago gun violence to racism in the porn industry. The writers even created a monthly segment called "CP Time," where I pontificated comedically over little-known Black history facts. One time we even shot a segment at T-Pain's house. Great guy. Only thing bigger than T-Pain's heart is his house.

Still, I don't know why not being able to do the Morris Brown story made me sad. It would be the last story I ever pitched that I really fought for. After that, I would email in pitches as usual, but I no longer allowed myself to become emotionally invested in anything that I pitched.

Emotionally uninvested is a very dangerous place to be.

Trevor Noah had announced a month or so before Georgia Week that he would be leaving the show at the end of the year. As always, I wanted good product on the screen for him, and we did good, hard work on Cop City. The piece aired in November of 2022 and was well received.

Trevor's last show was about six weeks away. I began to wonder if maybe it was time for me to start thinking about the big picture of what my life would be on the other side of this show.

Around that same time, I got a call from a colleague at Jackson State University, a Black college in Mississippi. She'd managed to pull off the unthinkable: She'd secured me an interview with then-head football coach Deion "Prime Time" Sanders. The NFL Hall of Famer was now in his second year coaching at this HBCU and the team, led by Deion's son Shedeur as quarterback, was demolishing their opponents on the way to winning their conference. Because of Deion, attendance was up. Black college football game organizers felt that enrollment at the institutions would spike as well. Deion's success was one of the biggest stories in sports that year. "Coach Prime," as the kids called him, was notoriously picky about media requests, but for whatever reason Coach Prime agreed to talk to me. "You can only get him for thirty minutes, Roy! Not a minute more!" she stressed to me. "But since you're coming all the way down here, I will also get you the president of our university. No topic is off the table. But it has to be in the next week or so, before school breaks for Christmas holiday."

This was an even better version of the Morris Brown pitch. I had the sitting president of the college that was at the epicenter of one of the largest stories in sports, and I also had an NFL Hall of Fame head coach.

I raced around the building telling my producers the good news. A traditional field piece can take anywhere from four to eight weeks to be properly planned and laid out before you are on the plane to cover the story. But there are certain circumstances (e.g., a Trump rally or a major national protest) where the show can assemble a camera crew to shoot something on less than a week's notice. I felt that booking Deion Sanders was one of those instances.

I'm not sure if people inside the building felt the same way. Maybe it was the logistics of planning a quick shoot so close to Thanksgiving, right as Trevor was leaving. Maybe it was trying to figure out where an interview with Deion Sanders would fit in to whatever *The Daily Show* was destined to become in January of 2023. I don't know. But what I do know is that I was disappointed because I felt like everyone thought this window to interview Coach Prime would be open for a while and we could just return to it when we had time.

About a month or so later, Deion Sanders resigned from Jackson State University and accepted a job at the University of Colorado. And my window to interview him closed. That one stung a little. But the truth of the matter was, just because you're successful at parodying the news, that does not mean that you have the resources to move like the actual news. Even if everyone in the building wanted to do the story, it was highly unlikely that we would've been able to get out the door on such short notice. In hindsight, it was the kind of opportunity I should've just financed myself and, if the show wanted to use it, seek reimbursement or just keep the footage for my own distribution.

The thing that sealed the deal for me is kind of laughable in hindsight.

With Trevor Noah out the door, in January of 2023, *The Daily Show* began having weekly guest hosts. A series of celebrities and actors rotated through with varying degrees of success. Some were just there to pass the time, fulfilling their dream like a Make-A-Wish kid, while some of the others saw the opportunity for what it was: a chance to audition for Trevor's job. I saw it as an opportunity to display every part of my comedic being that hadn't yet been seen on camera. I wasn't just guest-hosting *The Daily Show*, I was showcasing my skills to the world. My week wasn't until later in the year in April, so I had time to study the other hosts and decide what did and didn't work for me.

When it was my turn, I proposed an idea that I thought would be cool. At the beginning of the show, I would walk to the news desk instead of starting there already sitting, as every other guest host had done.

I knew that stylistically this would be something different than what had been tried over the last few months. So in the weeks leading up to my guest-hosting week, I spoke with all of the decision makers so that the idea wouldn't feel like it was out of left field on the day of. When my hosting week came. I rehearsed the entrance, and it came out just fine.

On the day of my first show, a few minutes before the start of the actual taping with the live audience, I was told that it would be preferred if I started the show already sitting down at the desk. It was explained to me that the desk had gravitas and that sitting already in command of the desk would suggest a posture that demanded more respect from the viewer. I believe the creative issue was that we were a news parody show and that if I came out and walked to the desk, maybe it would feel too much like a late-night talk show or something other than news parody.

I'll never know. Sometimes these requests come from inside the building, sometimes they come from the network. I didn't flinch at their request. I obliged and started the show from the news desk instead of walking to it.

There are far bigger grievances to have at the job than not having a few seconds of creative control. Again, I was bummed, but I wasn't mad. I just didn't feel like I was able to do everything that fulfilled me. And if I was going to start coming to work sad or frustrated or with any degree of disdain for a job that many consider the opportunity of a lifetime, then the best thing for me to do was to make space for the person who was destined to be in the job after me. That was the truth, and sometimes the truth is not sexy enough for a gossip headline.

But after my guest-hosting week, it was time to start thinking about what would be next for me after *The Daily Show*. A few weeks after my guest-hosting week, I was given the time I would need to think.

In the summer of 2023, there was a five-month writers' strike that shut down television production across the country, including on our show. By October it was time for everyone to go back to work, and Comedy Central reached out and asked if I would be interested in returning as a correspondent. At the time, the rumor was that Hasan Minhaj was going to be the host but the network had rescinded its offer to him. When they came to me and asked if I wanted to come back as a correspondent, I asked them how they'd approach looking for a host. I never got what I considered to be a solid answer from the network on how they would be conducting the new search. The country was heading into a presidential election, and I knew that 2024 would be a prime opportunity to launch a program. If I was ever going to have a chance of launching a new idea, it was going to be during the 2024 election cycle. The gamble ended up paying off, and seven months later I was hired by CNN to host an American remake of a popular British news satire show, *Have I Got News for You.*

I loved everyone at *The Daily Show,* but I knew if I stayed, one day I might end up on TV telling my equivalent of Chicken's Deion Sanders joke. It would be a joke structured in a way that had been perfectly fine to tell earlier in my trajectory, but it wouldn't challenge me anymore, wouldn't allow me to evolve.

As I said before, if it doesn't make me happy, I don't feel like I should be doing it. Morris Brown, Coach Prime, walking to the desk, then the weird contract talks and the host search—they all just kind of added up, I guess.

The Daily Show was, and remains, the gold standard of political satire. The behemoth that Jon Stewart built has been around for well over twenty-five years for a good reason. But I was starting to feel more and more like a chef at an Italian restaurant who keeps suggesting they add burritos to the menu. They're never going to add them. So I decided to leave. To do what and where? Not sure. All I knew was leaving was probably the correct first step.

Son, you will probably never remember it, but I took you with me the day I went to clean up my office. I did it on a Sunday afternoon because I knew the building would be empty and I wanted a quiet exit. You and I did one last lap around the building and I explained to you that I was leaving because it was time to find something else.

I have never really known what it's like to work a job that I am not comfortable with. I've loved every job I've had, at least while I was doing it, whether it was raking leaves in the fall in Alabama or slinging plates at Golden Corral or hosting a morning radio show. All of those jobs I left on my own accord or was fired from. I've never stayed at a job where I felt uncertainty; I do not know what to do with that emotion. I may not even have a plan of where I'm going to land next, but I know what might happen if I stay.

That look on Michael Roof's face in the supply room in Columbia, Missouri, has never left my mind. If I feel my mood changing at all within a workplace and I know that there's nothing I can do to change the circumstances, I have to leave.

I wish that Michael Roof could have realized that everything we're doing as stand-up comedians is just to bring more people out to see us live. I wish that he could have realized that the goal was never Hollywood. The goal was to find a way to reach strangers who loved you enough to see you anywhere on earth that you chose to show up. That is true success, to me at least, and he had that.

Of course, I have things I want for my career, but I've never tried to attach myself to one goal so deeply that if I do not achieve it, then I'm a failure. Anticipation of success can excite us, but it can also fuel the disappointment that drives us to a very dark place if we aren't careful. I will never know the true specific reasons why people like Chicken have killed themselves. But I do know one consistent thing, that none of them were happy.

And, son, whatever I do, for your sake and mine, I'm always going to do my best to be happy. Seek that for yourself as well.

A Letter to My Fathers

Dear Fathers,

As I've thought about the lessons I've learned from you, the most important thing that I've discovered is that no one person has taught me everything I've needed to know as a man, nor was it their job.

This book was a journey of self-discovery. Without me realizing it, it became a behavioral audit of where so many layers of my morality originated.

Everyone that my father ever touched professionally has found a way to reach me and tell me the lessons he instilled in them. In a lot of ways that is probably the most efficient way for me to get the best parts of him in his absence.

Beyond my biological father, there are so many men whom I just do not have the space to properly discuss in this book. But you should know that I appreciate how great you were to me. None of you owed me anything. Each of you taught me something.

I learned honor from drug dealers, who will send you the money they owe you immediately after they sell the drugs, and dishonor from disingenuous military recruiters, who will pressure you to join the service, through your own reservations, to help meet their quotas. I learned mercy from a judge who didn't lock me up but could have, and trust from a probation officer who could have kept me close to home but didn't—two of the only people I've encountered who understand that when you go around screaming "crime and punishment" you are forgetting the rehabilitative part of our penal system.

Few of you were from the expected places that society has set up for us to find so-called mentors. But you encouraged me, you gave me tough love, you galvanized my emotional armor. You changed my life.

While I couldn't possibly mention you all, including innumerable coaches and Boys Club mentors, I do have a few other fathers I'd like to thank here.

■ ■ ■

TO DR. JAMES HAWKINS:

In the 1970s, you introduced my parents to each other while the three of you were at Florida A&M University. You would eventually become the dean of the same FAMU school of journalism that gave me my degree in broadcast journalism. You were also one of the people who wrote a letter of recommendation to federal prosecutors, asking that I be given probation and not prison time. And then you turned right back around and wrote a letter of recommendation that my suspension from college not turn into an expulsion. You helped me get back on the right path.

■ ■ ■

TO MY HIGH SCHOOL BASEBALL COACH, LAWRENCE LOGAN:

Coach Logan, you wrote two of those letters as well. I wasn't very good at baseball, so that's why I'm grateful that you were the first person to give me an award that highlighted my hard work. Every year at the team banquet a player would be awarded the hustle award, and I won it my junior year. Generally, the player who worked the hardest wasn't the best player because the best players usually didn't work as hard. I was easily one of the three worst people on the team, so to have my hustle recognized was an honor.

I took a lot of pride in that award. It felt good to have someone look me in the eyes and simply say, "I see how hard you work, and I want you to know that you should keep going and keep pushing." That was a good day.

■ ■ ■

TO PASTOR THOMAS E. GILMORE:

Church wasn't a big part of my life growing up. The only pastor that ever really meant something to me was you, whom I remember from the First Baptist Ensley, which I attended for most of high school.

After my father died, you came to our house to pray with us. I never forgot that, because so few people came by our home at that time. My father had been in hospice at my brother's house, and since that's where he died, that was where most people went to pay their respects.

After I graduated college and came back to Birmingham, I was working the road as a comedian, so my churchgoing days were pretty much over. But every once in a while, I'd run into you in a random place in the city. The last time I saw you before you passed was across the aisle from me on a flight back to Birmingham from Atlanta in 2010. At the time I was performing at a fever pitch at colleges. It wasn't uncommon in an average month for me to perform in twenty to twenty-five different cities. Exhaustion oozed through my veins.

I guess you could see it on my face. You took one long look at me and said, "Son, you need a wife." I tried to laugh it off, but you were dead serious. You didn't say much more beyond that, but I knew you were saying that my pursuit of this thing I loved was purposeless without someone to pass that love to. I'm still unmarried as I write this. I'll simply say that you were probably right, Pastor Gilmore. I'll get to it someday. I'll get to it sooner or later.

■ ■ ■

TO ARSENIO HALL:

One time, back in 2003, I was on CBS's *Star Search,* and I didn't like the ratings that the judges gave me. Most of the judges who had loved me the first week hated me the second and gave me one star out of five. I brought my mic to my mouth to curse at them and you just gently tugged on the cuff of my jacket to keep me from doing it—all while talking with the judges and hosting a live television show. When we went to commercial break, you turned to me and just mumbled under your breath, "Nobody will remember a bad joke. Everybody will remember a bad attitude."

A two-inch motion from your hand saved me from being a lifetime internet joke. It would be almost twenty years later to the day when *The Daily Show* won an Emmy and I ran into you backstage congratulating Trevor Noah. It was the first time I'd seen you since 2003 on *Star Search.* I shook your hand and told you thank you.

■ ■ ■

TO TREVOR NOAH:

Speaking of you, Trevor, I believe that there are people you learn from simply through observation. I saw firsthand that hosting a show like *The Daily Show* is like weathering a repeating series of storms. There are storms within the building, and there are storms within the news cycle, and there are also storms of backlash to how you cover said news. I don't think I've ever met someone calmer in a storm than you.

■ ■ ■

TO BUCK WILDE (AKA SAMUEL MACK):

As the *Morning Show* host I eventually succeeded at 95.7 Jamz, Buck Wilde (aka Samuel Mack), you taught me that you have to make something as good as you think it needs to be, not what other people think it should be, because most other people's bar is going to be lower than yours.

You were a fair man who sometimes needed some persuading to try an idea, but you were always open to experimentation and listened to other people on your show. You never pretended to have all the right answers, but you would always question your approach. You taught me what it meant to do my best work.

■ ■ ■

TO WILLIAM E. GILMORE:

People will sometimes ask me, who was my mentor? It's a very difficult question for me to answer. There is no single man to point to, and to be honest, I'm glad that there isn't. I feel blessed and fortunate to have lived a life that has allowed me to cross paths with so many amazing people. Also, some of the moments, albeit profound, were extremely brief. The closest I came to having a mentor was with you, William, and even that was just for the first two years that I did stand-up.

Your career as a stand-up comedian was on the rise when I first started doing comedy in Tallahassee. I met you literally the second time I ever told a joke on stage. You saw enough in me to allow me to shadow you on a few gigs that year, and I'm forever grateful for that. I performed here and there with you, but you let me ride with you to watch the vibes of the show, to watch you go over your notes, and to watch your approach to shaping the show. Then, on the three-hour ride back to Tallahassee, we'd analyze your set. No matter how well you did, you were never comfortable with it. There was always something that could be improved. I respected that work ethic considering that you were also a schoolteacher during the day.

You were a married father of two, and the most important thing I learned from you was a lesson that I wouldn't be able to apply until my son was born. I used to look at staying home instead of being on the road as a burden. But now, as much as I love doing this shit, I know that there's nothing more important than raising your children and being there for them. I shudder at the thought of having to leave New York City for more than a few days at a time. I understand what you were feeling, Gilmore. Men who have family have a different smile than men who have success. I hope to have a Gilmore smile one day.

■ ■ ■

TO YOU, MY SON:

Which brings me to you, my son. My life has been a quiet journey of hopscotching from person to person, gleaning nuggets from them. I'm very lucky to have had them all in my life. And the most recent father in my life—the most recent person to teach me what it means to be a dad, to be a man—is you.

You're not going to learn everything you need to learn from me. I can give you as much as I can, but I can only hope that you will have as many fathers as I have. I've been blessed to live a life filled with people who have treated me based on their belief of who I could become and not solely off of who I was at the time. May you always see yourself through the same lens of positivity and potential. And may you always see other people through that lens and treat them accordingly.

Love,
Roy

Acknowledgments

They told me this is a place where I'm supposed to make acknowledgments and mention people that I hold dear. I got love for my mom, my son, and his mother.

It would be impossible to name anyone else without forgetting someone and having someone feel slighted. I don't want that pressure. Also a little-known fact about book publishing is that acknowledgments are usually done last, after you were mentally exhausted from writing an entire book.

Also, Kashmir Thompson, thank you for using your brilliant artistry to bring images to these stories. I'm also sorry for calling you at the very last minute, but you are a very good artist and I figured you could handle the tight deadline and you did not prove me wrong.

ABOUT THE AUTHOR

ROY WOOD JR. is a two-time Emmy-nominated writer and producer. The comedian, actor, and podcaster is primarily known for his stand-up comedy and work as a correspondent on Comedy Central's *The Daily Show* and hosting CNN's *Have I Got News for You*. He hosted the 2023 White House Correspondents' dinner and the 85th Peabody Awards. He has created original half-hour scripted projects at FOX, NBC, and Comedy Central. He is the former host of the award-winning Comedy Central podcast *The Daily Show: Beyond the Scenes*. He remains a regular guest star on various ESPN shows and the MLB Network. Roy lives in New York.